DYING FOR ANOTHER DAY

DYING FOR ANOTHER DAY

PETE EDRIS AND RAYMOND REID

authorHOUSE®

AuthorHouse™
1663 Liberty Drive
Bloomington, IN 47403
www.authorhouse.com
Phone: 1-800-839-8640

First published by AuthorHouse 10/29/2011

ISBN: 978-1-4520-2300-7 (sc)
ISBN: 978-1-4520-2301-4 (hc)
ISBN: 978-1-4520-2299-4 (ebk)

Library of Congress Number: 2010907203

Printed in the United States of America
Bloomington, Indiana

This book is printed on acid-free paper.

INTRODUCTION

RAYMOND REID

Men who manned B-17 Flying Fortress bombers in World War II were not men at all, but twenty-one and twenty-two year old boys. Hundreds of these brave airmen served in the 306th Bombardment Group that was established on Jan. 28, 1942. It was activated on March 8, 1942.

The 306th a division of the Mighty 8th Air Force completed 300 missions over Occupied Europe and Nazi Germany. The 306th was the first USAAF heavy bomb group to attack a strategic target located in Nazi Germany when the group attacked Wilhelmshaven; an attack led by Colonel Frank A. Armstrong on Jan. 27, 1943. Colonel Armstrong's experiences with the 97th and 306th Bomb Groups became the basis of Sy Bartlett and Beirne Lay, Jr.'s novel and movie, "Twelve O'clock High."

On January 1, 1943, First Lieutenant Pete Edris was transferred to the 306th Bomb Group, 369th Bomb Squad, and served under Col. Armstrong (who was portrayed by Gregory Peck in the movie).

This is Pete's story. It's a story of a twenty-two year old boy whose B-17 bomber was blown out of the sky over Rennes, France, on March 8, 1943. It's a story about the people who befriended him. And it's a testimonial to his irrepressible desire to survive one of Nazi Germany's most notorious prison camps, Stalag Luft III, from where the "The Great Escape" was based. It's a story about living to see another day . . . and reuniting with Doris Cooke, his soul mate . . . and the love of his life.

It's a truly remarkable story about a rare World War II statistic: An infinitesimal twenty-three American soldiers were declared dead in World War II . . . and lived to tell about it.

Pete Edris was one of those soldiers. And this is his unforgettable story.

ACKNOWLEDGEMENT

PETE EDRIS

I dedicate this book to the brave 8th Air Force flight crews who lost their lives during World War II in the European Theatre of Operations.

CONTENTS

I

PREPARING FOR TAKEOFF

In 1937 I was just a little guy in a little high school in Mountain Lakes, New Jersey. (Little meaning I was about 4' 11" and could not participate in sports.) Although Yankee Stadium was practically next-door in The Bronx, New York, I had no aspirations of becoming the next Babe Ruth or Lou Gehrig. My ambitions were lofty in a sense though: I wanted to be a pilot. Movies such as "Wings," "I Wanted Wings," and the "Ace Drummond" serials with Lon Chaney, Jr. gave me the fever. And although "Wings" was a World War I movie, I knew little about the war, except what little I had learned in school. Neither did I know about the Nazi Party and Adolph Hitler's Third Reich and what they were up to, even as I sat in the theatre in Boonton, New Jersey-about two miles from Mountain Lakes. I had never heard of a B-17 either, or the prototype that was tested on July 28, 1935 at Wright Field in Dayton, Ohio. Being an airplane fanatic, however, I did know that Wright Field, which became Wright Patterson Field in 1948, was named after the Wright Brothers, Wilbur and Orville. Dayton always claimed "ownership" to the birth of flight, but North Carolina begged to differ. The first flight was successfully launched there at Kitty Hawk, on December 17, 1903.

The army ordered its first batch of B-17s in 1938, thirteen to be exact. Sitting in the theatre that day I couldn't imagine what the future held for me, or how a B-17 would end up shaping my life.

I was only seventeen years old so Hitler, Nazi Germany and B-17s were not even on my radar screen; at least not yet.

I just wanted to learn how to fly. There were a few very small airlines in those days, and I wanted to fly for one of them.

My parents couldn't afford private lessons so they sent me to a junior college, which was a prerequisite (along with being at least twenty years old) for aviation cadet training

The college we decided on was Oak Ridge Military Institute in tiny Oak Ridge, North Carolina. Oak Ridge was located between Greensboro and Winston-Salem and about seven miles east of the sleepy little town of Kernersville. My parents drove me down from Mountain Lakes in late August of 1938 in our '37 Dodge. I remember stopping and spending the night along the way. I think it was at a hotel in downtown Richmond, Virginia.

Oak Ridge was established in 1852 by the Society of Friends (Quakers) as a "finishing school" for boys. It became one of the best prep schools in North Carolina and was well known for its debating societies as well as its athletics. Oak Ridge teams regularly played the likes of Wake Forest, the University of North Carolina and Trinity College (later Duke University).

In 1929 Oak Ridge officially became an all-male military secondary school as well as a junior college. During World War II, 127 of the academy's alumni were awarded the Purple Heart while another twenty-seven earned the Silver Star. It's ironic that Oak Ridge became a military school after being formed by Quakers, who are devout pacifists.

Today, Oak Ridge is the third-oldest military school in the United States still in operation.

A lot of boys were (and still are) sent to Oak Ridge for disciplinary reasons. The code of conduct there was very strict. It was early to bed and early to rise with absolutely no room for "monkey business." There was room, however, for initiation rites, or hazing, which included having my rear end beaten around pretty good by the second year guys.

One of their initiation methods included a large, wooden paddle with holes in it. They called it the "Board of Education" and it worked very well. My rear end was sore all year. Another technique they used involved a toothbrush. They would make me drop my drawers and they would take that toothbrush and kind of rub it back and forth on my butt, in the same spot, until a blister was created. Didn't hurt my growth, though. At Oak Ridge I grew almost five inches to about 5' 5." My mother had taken me to a doctor in Mountain Lakes who prescribed some type of growth pill. To this day I don't know what it was. But they worked. Or they were just placebos that helped get my mind off my inferior height. Didn't matter, though. I ended up becoming about the average height for a grown man in the 1940s: 5'8."

A couple of my buddies at Oak Ridge in 1938

All of us at Oak Ridge had to perform "guard duty" at one time or another in front of the school. It was a boring job except for that one fateful Saturday afternoon in September of 1938. That was the day a Model A Ford pulled up to the curb loaded with a bunch of giggling girls. Needless to say, I deserted my post, walked over, and struck up a conversation. But before I could get my first sentence out one of the girls exclaimed, "Why . . . it's a damn Yaaankee!" The girl turned out to be Doris Cooke, a petite blue-eyed brunette and the cutest girl I'd ever laid eyes on. I learned that she was a sophomore at Kernersville High School and lived in the middle of town. We didn't have that many dates when I was at Oak Ridge because I didn't have a car and she didn't have a license. Plus, Oak Ridge had very strict rules for off campus trips and an early curfew of 11:00 p.m. So our only dates were meeting for Cokes in Kernersville - and I had to walk seven miles to get there. We met at Pinnix Drug Store, a Kernersville institution. It's where you bought all your sundries and had your prescriptions filled while you sat at the soda counter and enjoyed a Coke or a milkshake. The Cokes were five cents and the milk shakes were a quarter. Meeting for Cokes was about the extent of Doris' and my "love life" during my two years at Oak Ridge. We would soon go our separate ways, me back to New Jersey and she to wherever. I told Doris that whatever happened, I would never forget her. "I will never forget you, either, Pete Edris," she said. "After all, you're the first boy who ever kissed me . . . and a damn Yankee, at that!"

Back at Oak Ridge that night I couldn't get Doris off my mind. Would we stay in touch as we promised? Or just grow apart over time.

Something deep down, though, told me that this was not just a passing fancy.

2

FLYING HIGH IN MISSISSIPPI

After Oak Ridge I worked in New York as an office boy. My father was an insurance investigator and probably wanted me to follow in his footsteps. But I hated "office" work and couldn't wait until I was twenty and eligible for flight school.

And it finally happened: On August 29, 1941, I went to 90 Church Street in New York City and was sworn in as an aviation cadet in the Army Air Corps. From there we were put on a train bound for Montgomery, Alabama. We were the first class to be called "Aviation Cadets." The previous title was "Flying Cadets." We also were the first class to have preflight training before we ever got into an airplane. Ground school included all kinds of stuff, including mathematics and meteorology. Thanks to my military training at Oak Ridge, this all came very easy for me. I really had a good time because hazing was as easy as a cakewalk. The upperclassmen couldn't even touch me without my permission. They could do little more than straighten my tie or my nameplate. What a relief to know they couldn't beat me like the guys at Oak Ridge did.

My next step after Montgomery was primary flight school, where I flew PT 17s in Jackson, Mississippi. The PT 17 was a Stearman biplane with two open cockpits. The instructor sat in front and a cadet sat in back. We had sixty hours there, before we went to basic training. Each school lasted about eight weeks. There were four weeks as underclassmen and four weeks as upperclassmen at each school. Four of us (Campbell, Bader, Jones and me) were assigned to a guy named Ted Woodbeck. He was shorter than me because I had made it to 5' 8." And he was quite a pilot. His training went all the way back to the twenties and early thirties when he was a crop duster. He was the guy who really taught me how to fly. You really had to know the mechanics of an airplane to fly a biplane. I kept wanting to grab the stick with my left hand because I'm left handed. But Woodbeck grabbed my left hand and said, "That hand goes on the throttle (which is on the left) and you put your RIGHT hand on the stick." I was thinking I might flunk out before I got off the ground! But as it turned out, all four of us passed with flying colors. But this success didn't bode well for our future, though. Campbell had his head blown off, Bader also was killed, Jones was wounded . . . and we'll get to me later. Not much of a track record, huh?

*Showing off my uniform
in primary flight school*

*Ted Woodbeck, my flight
instructor in Jackson, Miss.*

The first ten hours of flight training consisted of normal maneuvers. I was told how to bank left and right . . . and climb and descend. Instructors weren't allowed to do any acrobatics until you had ten hours. Then they could put you on your back. One day he used a Gosport tube to communicate with me. It was sort of like a stethoscope. I had a helmet on and the tubes to the Gosports – a tube in each ear in my helmet. I could hardly hear a word Woodbeck said. The wind was screaming in each side of my helmet.

L-R: Instructor Woodbeck, me, Bader, Jones and Campbell

I was certain that he was going to put me on my back, as in he was going to roll it over, upside down. So . . . I grabbed the seat with both hands. He asked, "You got your seatbelt on?" I shook my head up and down, yes. He had a mirror and every time he asked a question, he looked in the mirror to see if I understood. I couldn't talk back. So I grabbed the bottom of the seat on each side as hard as

I could. We rolled over on our backs and he said, "All right Edris, let me see your hands." I shook my head sideways, no. "Damnit, Edris, I'll wash you out if I don't see your hands." (He was yelling so loud I could actually hear him over the wind). I let go of that seat and stuck my hands up to my shoulders. He yelled, "Stick 'em way out!" I ended up just hanging by my seatbelt. Of course I was wearing a parachute, but I was terrified nonetheless.

After the war people often asked me if I ever practiced bailing out of airplanes. The answer was "no." We didn't even read a book on how to bail out. All they told us was where the ripcord handle was. That's all they ever told us. Period.

But at least on this day of flying upside down, I didn't have to bail out. Hoped I wouldn't have to bail out during my first solo flight either. But I'd soon find out. You believe you're never ready for your first solo, they say. Well, they're right. And my primary instructor wasn't very encouraging either when he said: "Edris, go kill yourself; because I sure as hell won't be on that airplane. You're on your on. That's why they call it 'solo.'"

The PT-17 trainer and me

Well, I took off and let out a whoop. We had check points to let us know where to make our downwind leg, where to turn onto the base leg, and where to turn for the final approach. The last thing the instructor said before he got off the wing was, "If you bounce too hard and your nose goes up in the air, just remember to stick and throttle; the stick forward and throttle forward to full power. Go on around and make another try." So . . . I came down the first time and bounced onto the ground. All I could remember was, "stick and throttle." I gave it full power and went around and did the exact same thing the second time. I went around a third time thinking if I was going to get this bird down alive! I was so mad on this third try that I came down and just pulled the stick back into my belly and let the thing come down. It bounced along the ground like a big rubber ball. I could see the instructor frantically waving his arms. I taxied over and he said, with great relief: "Okay. I think that'll do it for today, Edris." Well . . . I passed (sigh of relief).

But right before my graduation, something horrible happened at Pearl Harbor. And the world would never be the same.

At 7:58 a.m. on December 7, 1941, a sneak attack was executed by the Japanese Navy on the U.S. Pacific Fleet in Pearl Harbor. Japan's objective was to cripple the fleet and keep it from interfering with its plans to wage war in Southeast Asia against Britain, the Netherlands, and the U.S.

The attack was devastating. The bombings killed more than 2,300 Americans. They completely destroyed the U.S.S. Arizona, capsized the U.S.S. Oklahoma, sank three other ships and demolished 180 aircraft.

President Roosevelt called December 7, 1941, "A date which will live in infamy." The attack was the catalyst for America to enter the war with all its might, not only in the Pacific, but also in Europe, where Nazi Germany and Imperial Italy had declared war on the United States and its allies.

I knew in my heart that the war would affect my buddies and me more than we ever could imagine. It would change everything: Our plans, our hopes . . . our dreams.

I felt my appointment with destiny was drawing near. I had no idea where I would meet my fate. But I knew it wouldn't be in Mountain Lakes, New Jersey.

3

EARNING MY WINGS

After graduation from primary flight school we went on to basic training in Greenville, Mississippi, which is right on the Mississippi River. There was a new field there and we were its inaugural class. I liked the place except for one thing: Lack of food. For the first couple of weeks I thought I was going to starve. About all we had to eat was chipped beef on toast. In the military, this "delicacy" became known as S.O.S, "shit on a shingle!" There I was introduced to a Vultee BT 13A. It was a low-wing monoplane with a fixed, non-retractable landing gear. It had a radio (which I quickly learned how to use) and an intercom in the cockpit.

The Vultee BT-13A in Greenville, Miss.

In Greenville I had a screaming instructor who was louder than Woodbeck. This guy would actually beat his head on the instrument panel when I did something wrong. Finally, it was time for me to solo. The first day up I remember it was very cold. I mean . . . it was cold even by New Jersey standards (and this was the deep south!). It was so cold that on my first landing attempt the wing stalled out because of frost. So I just crunched it down onto the runway. My instructor pulled the plane over to a side taxi strip and left the engine running. Then he jumped down and actually put his shoulder under the wing, lifted it up and down, and looked at the strut to see if it was damaged.

Vultee BT-13A instrument panel

Meanwhile, I'm looking out the side of the cockpit, wondering what the hell he was doing! Then, lo and behold, he goes to the other wing and checks it out too by lifting it with his shoulder. I thought who does this guy think he is, Charles Atlas? Then he climbed up onto the wing and hollered in my face, "Okay, Edris, you're going solo."

Well, "I must be doing something right," I thought. And I guess I was, because I went on to pass my solo test with flying colors.

At the wheel of a riverboat, Greenville, Miss.

After graduating from basic I went to twin engine - advanced training at Columbus Army Flying School in Columbus, Mississippi. We were actually the first class there, too. We trained on two airplanes. One was a little AT8 Cessna. The other plane was a Lockheed Hudson, which the British were using for submarine patrol. It was a large, twin-engine plane with a twin tail. It was one of the most difficult planes that any of us ever flew. Several cadets got killed trying.

April 28, 1942 was my graduation day; the day I got my wings. And I was thrilled that my mother and two sisters, Helen and Lucille, showed up for the ceremony.

Graduation day with my friend, R. E. Jones

So here I was - a once 4' 11" high school runt who was too small to play any sport . . . showing off his wings. "I'll show you someday," I always said. And I did show 'em. Now I was a full-fledged second lieutenant with a pilot rating.

Showing off our wings as full-fledged second lieutenants with pilot rating.
L-R, C.J. Kelly, me and Paul Landt

My sister Helen and me on graduation day

By this time, Doris was college a student at Greensboro, N. C. And although we had been corresponding off and on through my cadet days, the relationship wasn't all that serious (I didn't think). But when she told me how hurt she was that I hadn't invited her to my graduation, I knew I had screwed up. I knew from then on that I'd be more sensitive to her feelings.

4

MY DATE WITH THE "FLYING FORTRESS"

After graduation it was time to move on to McDill Field in Tampa, Florida for B-17 training. When I found out we were going into four-engine bombers, I thought, "Lord God, I'm going to wash out. I'll never learn to fly those behemoths!" Compared to the bi-plane I learned to fly on, this was like jumping from the Little League to the Major Leagues. No wonder they called this thing the "Flying Fortress." It was 70 feet long and weighed almost 40,000 pounds; that's before you added the ten-man crew, almost 6,000 pounds of bombs and several thousand pounds of fuel. The wingspan was a gigantic 104 feet and the plane was powered by four 1,200 horsepower radial engines. No wonder these engines were named "Wright Cyclone" radials. Because that's what they sounded like: Cyclones! So here I am: a twenty-one year old kid learning how to fly a 40,000 - pound bomber that cost $276,000. Yikes! What have I gotten myself into? But we found out that these birds were very forgiving. That you could make a million mistakes and still bring it home. And they could take quite a beating, too. They were like Timex watches claimed to be in their 1950s advertising: They would "Take a Lickin' and Keep on Tickin."

Painting I did of a B-17 'Flying Fortress'

13

We spent about a month at McDill, where we were assigned to the 92nd Bomb Group. Then we moved further south to Sarasota, Florida for combat training. Because America had declared war only five months before, everything was new, which meant there was no defined training schedule. You might say we were sort of flying by the seat of our pants. All the while, though, we were preparing to go to England to join forces with the 8th Air Force and the Royal Air Force (RAF) for battle in the European Theatre of Operations (ETO).

Me at Lido Beach in Sarasota, Florida   *Partying at Lido Beach.*
That's me in the foreground

We flew all day, every day that summer of 1942. We learned high-altitude flying (25,000 feet), bombing, navigation . . . everything. Pilots also had to check out some of the gun positions: There were two nose guns operated by the bombardier, two tail guns, two belly (ball turret guns,) a side nose gun for the navigator, two waist guns, and the twin top turret guns operated by the flight engineer. Each of these guns was a .50 caliber machine gun, designed to blow enemy fighters out of the sky: In the ETO we will be the target of Me-109s, designed by famed German aeroplane designer Willy Messerschmitt. With a top speed of 379 mph, we'll have to blow it out of the sky, because we sure as hell can't outrun it. The other Nazi fighter that will have us in its crosshairs will be the FW (Focke-Wulf) – 190. One squadron of FW-190s was nicknamed "Yellow Nose," because the cowlings around the engine were painted yellow. This was no slouch of a fighter plane, either. Powered by a BMW 14-cylinder radial engine, its top speed was 395 mph.

So . . . that's what I had to look forward to. And it was going to be sooner than later - because around August 15, 1942, I was on a ship heading for England.

5

BON VOYAGE

They put me on a ship called the U.S.S. West Point, formerly called the America. It was one of the few ocean liners around at that time, but now it was a troop ship. And it was jam-packed . . . probably to the tune of several thousand men. It was so crowded that some guys were sleeping in empty swimming pools. As a second lieutenant, I was afforded a stateroom, but it was no "bargain," because six of us were crammed into a room designed for two. Our ship was part of the first big convoy to leave America for England. In that convoy there was a World War I battleship, several cruisers, some destroyers, and several supply ships.

It took us two weeks to get to England because we had to zigzag all over the place to avoid German submarines. We docked in Liverpool and I'll never forget my first impression of the British: I thought they all looked alike. In America everybody seemed different. But here I just felt that everybody looked just like everybody else.

Anyhow . . . we got off the ship and took a troop train to Bovington, which is north of London. The 92nd was the third B-17 group to arrive in England, and we received a nasty shock: We were turned into the "Combat Crew Replacement Center (CCRC)." Basically, that meant we would be used to "re -supply" crews that had been injured, captured, or killed. In other words, my buddies and I were to be shipped out one at a time as needed. This was a real morale killer, because we would no longer be a cohesive group.

Our barracks in Bovington were called Nissin huts – steel buildings with a rounded roof. There were ten to twelve of us in one hut. And the huts and barracks were spread out all over the place because of possible German bomb raids. We were so spread out that it was too far to get anywhere by foot. To get to anywhere . . . operations, mess hall officer's club and even the airplanes . . . we rode bikes lent to us by the British. But I went one better: I bought a BMW motorcycle from a guy--- dirt- cheap. I think I paid about ten pounds for it, which was probably about fifty bucks back then. It was probably stolen or something, but I didn't care. I kept it until I was transferred and gave it away to some guy I just met on the street.

For some reason, at least back then, there was never any ice anywhere, seemingly in all of England. But we came up with an idea. On party nights in the officer's club, we'd put several cases of beer on a B-17 and take it up to 25,000 feet. At that altitude it was about forty below zero, so it didn't take long for our beer to get cold. Not the most efficient use of a B-17, but it sure as hell beat drinking warm beer! And beer drinking was about all the social life we had; except for two days leave a month. On those days it was "London here we come!" We always went to Piccadilly Circus and stayed at the Piccadilly Hotel. And every time we walked in we could see the managers start wringing their hands. The first thing I did at the hotel was head for the barbershop. Back then you could get the "whole works" for a pound. By "works" I mean haircut, shave, hair wash, and even a manicure.

The blacked-out streets of London were crazy in those days and hookers were everywhere. Streetwalkers would walk up and say, "Yank, would you like to be naughty tonight?" We joked among ourselves that you'd better light up a cigarette near their faces to see if they had any running sores!

But most of us knew better than to fool around with these women. If you did, you had to use protection. No one could leave base without a "Pro (prophylactic) Kit." It was absolutely mandatory. As for me, it seemed that the more women I was around the more I missed Doris. Our letters had been more frequent lately, and more intense. I wondered how Cokes at a corner drug store in a little town in North Carolina could lead to what was happening. Our "keep in touch" letters had become "I really miss you" letters and now . . . full-blown love letters. We even talked about marriage.

I brought her last letter along to the Piccadilly and read it over and over before I went to sleep.

My Darling,

I am still working pretty hard and am dying to see you. As I sit here and listen to Jimmy Simms sing I feel like having a big cry. Oh! My Goodness. Jimmy Simms is singing "Good night wherever you are."

Darling, I do love you more every minute and I'd give the world to think that I could see you tonight. I'll be the happiest girl in the world when we can be married and you can come home every night.

Honey, I took some more pictures Sunday so I'll have some to mail you in a day or so. I hope you have gotten some of the others that I have sent you.

Well, sweetheart, I must close now, but I'll write tomorrow. Goodnight, hon. I love you with all my heart and soul, and I miss you so much.

All my love,

Doris

The very next day I wrote her a letter and asked her to marry me. It was official: We had become engaged "by proxy." My mother picked out a 1/2 – carat diamond engagement ring and sent it to Doris. I just hoped and prayed that I'd live to put it on her finger.

On January 1, 1943, I was transferred from the 11th CCRC to the 306th Bomb Group, 369 Bomb Squadron. It was called the Fightin'-Bitin' squad. I had checked out at Bovington as a full-fledged Aircraft Commander. And luckily, for my welfare, Major Terry, the 369th Commander, said, "We're going to give your crew to an experienced co-pilot who's flown ten missions. He's going to pilot your crew and you're going to take his place as a co-pilot for ten missions. Then you'll get a replacement crew that comes in later."

Since I was so very inexperienced, this sounded like a good plan to me.

I was assigned to First Lieutenant Robert "Rip" Riordan and I felt downright intimidated. I'd been reading about him in the *Stars and Stripes,* our Armed Forces newspaper and about the airplanes he had flown. He brought one back that was so damaged that the only thing they could use it for was spare parts. His planes had been shot up all over the place. He had been shot, his navigator had been hit, and his co-pilot had been wounded. He was almost bigger than life. Plus, he was the most self-disciplined man I had ever met. He didn't drink, smoke or swear. And he never went out with women. Even on his days off he avoided leaving the base for London or anywhere else. Afraid he might miss a mission. It seemed as if Riordan was born to fly combat.

*First Lieutenant Robert "Rip" Riordan celebrating his 25ᵗʰ mission. Riordan would later
become a Lieutenant Colonel and complete an astounding 41 missions*

I had heard he was a stickler for details, including keeping the equipment clean. That was reinforced the first time I met him when he said, "Edris, let's go out to the airplane. And the first thing we'll do is making sure it's clean. A clean plane flies better. Don't ever forget that, lieutenant. A clean plane flies better."

Riordon pretty much had his own rules and most of them didn't include emergency procedures. "I don't need emergency procedures because I'm not bailing out of the airplane, "he exclaimed. "If it's flyable – even going down – we're going to fly it, right to the last possible minute. When the Germans see you and you are up high and you bail out, they can see you for miles. They will know exactly where you are when you hit the ground. If we get shot down, then, we're going to go down to tree top level and coast as far as we can then crash land. That way we'll be well away from where anybody last saw us."

Riordon volunteered for more than twenty-five missions and ended up doing forty-one, which was unheard of. All you had to do were twenty-five and you went home. And that rarely happened. Most crews never completed even fifteen.

It was all beginning to seem surreal. I think the worst part I feared was the unknown. I was a twenty-two year old kid and all I could do was trust my superiors and do what they told me to do; co-pilot the plane to wherever the hell they told us to go, drop the payload of bombs; and try to get the plane and crew back in one piece. I may have been young, but I knew one thing: this wasn't a backyard game of cowboys and Indians. It was war and it was real. If our Allies and we couldn't cripple Hitler and the Third Reich, we sure as hell would die trying.

Hopefully all of us in the 306th were committed to what we were supposed to be doing. But something didn't seem right. There was no feeling of being on a team here at all. Morale was really bad. And the group was losing B-17s left and right. The 306th became the inspiration for the novel, "Twelve O'clock High," by Sy Bartlett and Beirne Lay, Jr., and later, the award-winning movie starring Gregory Peck as Colonel Frank A. Savage. In real life, Savage was Colonel Frank A. Armstrong whom I served under in the 306th.

Armstrong was just as intimidating as Gregory Peck. The first day he was assigned to our group he called all the combat crews to the briefing hut. He got up on stage and told us off pretty good. He told us to quit feeling sorry for ourselves. He said this was a shooting war and that some of us were going to get killed. He said he had been sent here to take over what was being called "A hard luck group." "Well, I don't believe in hard luck," he said, "So we're going to find out what's going wrong and why. You're worrying too much. You're worrying about the future when you may not even have one.

"Stop thinking about going home . . . because you may never go home. **You might as well consider yourself already dead.** And if you're not tough enough to understand what I'm talking about, I don't want you in this group."

A sergeant in the back stood up and said, "Sir, part of our problem is we're going on missions hungry. We get up in the morning and there is nothing to eat. And by the time we returned from our missions, all the food is gone. We have to scrounge around for ourselves." A lot of guys, including me, got up and started clapping. On many mornings I had to heat a piece of bread on a potbellied stove, and maybe get a cup of coffee. And that was about it. The mess hall guys just weren't getting up in time to fix us anything.

Armstrong's face turned bright red. "Sergeant," he said, "Go bring me the mess sergeant and the mess officer right this minute." When they got there Armstrong ripped into them, which went against Army rules. Officers aren't supposed to be chewed out in public. He busted the sergeant to a private, right there on the spot. I believe the mess officer was later court martialled.

The next day Armstrong made it clear. "When our planes take off on a mission, nobody eats until the crews get back. And when they finish eating, the rest of the Group can eat and drink." So . . . we finally had food before a mission, and were the first to eat after a mission.

He also instituted another "custom:" A shot of booze after each mission. Everybody got a shot. We immediately went looking for guys who didn't drink so we could get their shots.

Some guys got lucky and ended up with three or even four shots. Morale was getting better already.

But every mission had its moments. On my first mission after Armstrong arrived Riordan and I found gun trouble during preflight checks. One of the two waist guns wasn't working and one of the tail guns wasn't working; but headstrong Riordan was going anyway. We were the last bomber scheduled for takeoff, and we were all taxiing, one behind the other. Once we were cleared for takeoff we'd go up in thirty-second intervals. B-17s carried a large bomb load, at least 5,000 pounds (five-1,000 pounders, or ten-500 pounders. Add fuel, and a B-17's total weight was over 60,000 pounds. And we had only a 5,000-foot runway on which to take off. And it took every foot to get these birds off the ground.

As we were heading for takeoff that day the engineer ran up and screamed to Riordan, "Sir, one of the waist gunners just jumped off the plane. He's not going, and I don't want to go either."

As co-pilot, I felt the need to speak up, too: "I don't think we should go either, Rip. It's not fair to the crew to be up there without all of our guns."

Riordan, gritting his teeth, pulled the throttle back and turned the plane up on a side taxiway, parked it and cut off the engines. He was madder than hell!

18

As the jeeps from operations and maintenance started pulling up, Riordan got in the navigator's face and yelled, "Get up in the nose and figure out how long we can stay on the ground and still catch the Group." We weren't allowed to rejoin the Group if the other planes were halfway or more across the English Channel. The navigator came back and told Riordan that we couldn't stay on the ground for more than twenty minutes. As it turned out twenty minutes went by, then thirty . . . then forty. They couldn't fix the guns.

Back at the base, Riordan and I went into squadron operations and told Major Terry what happened. It was determined that the flight wasn't aborted, because the wheels never left the ground. An aborted mission would have been a disgrace to Riordan so he seemed somewhat relieved.

But he wasn't through with the waist gunner, however. He asked Major Terry what happens when a crew member deserts an aircraft when it's about to take off. "Oh, I don't know," said Terry. "I guess we could court martial him, or take him out and shoot him!"

Riordan turned the waist gunner in for something less serious and they busted him back to a private. Part of his punishment was he had to walk around the field with his parachute on-every day. It was humiliating. And every time he saw Riordan he literally got on his knees and begged to be put back on the crew. Finally Riordan, seeing that this guy was truly contrite, had him bumped back to a sergeant (you had to be at least a sergeant to fly) and reinstated him to the crew as a waist gunner.

Riordan was a control freak. He wouldn't let me touch anything. But I didn't blame him. He didn't know anything about me, or my flying ability. Finally, he gave me a little something to do. On a January 13 mission he let me handle the throttles and all the other knobs and levers to keep us in formation. Since this was a six or seven hour mission, it took some of the strain off of him. It was on that mission that the FW-190 came right at us from 1:00 O'clock. I pulled off my oxygen mask and yelled to Riordan, "God . . . his wings are on fire!" Then I wrapped my hands around my head to protect myself. That's when Riordan broke out laughing and said, "His wings aren't on fire, that's his 20 millimeters firing. Plus, when they're aiming at us, they're actually shooting at the guy behind us."

After that mission he gained some trust in me and we both started flying the airplane. And we never flew a mission that something didn't hit us. That was the problem with daylight bombing. We were sitting ducks for the 88- millimeter ground fire. They fired shrapnel (called flack) all over the place. Also, some of the guns jettisoned their empty shells overboard when they fired. This was like flying in a golf ball-size hailstorm. We'd duck and push the plane up, down and all over the place trying to get out of the way. Some of the B-17s actually had their Plexiglas noses damaged by the empty shells.

I remember one of the shells actually sticking to the edge of the wing on my side. It stayed there the whole mission. It didn't fall off until our final approach home.

Another day. Another mission. And another shot of whiskey!

The night before my next mission I didn't stop with just one shot of whiskey; or two, either. My navigator, bombardier and I went into Bedford to a place called the Officers' Key club. I got drunk as a dog. When we got back to the base they had to put me to bed (I was passed out), but not before they shaved off exactly half of my moustache.

I got up so late for the mission the next morning that I didn't even have time to wash my face. So I rushed down to the briefing and wondered why everyone was laughing at me. My navigator and bombardier buddies were afraid I'd be pissed, but I actually thought it was hilarious. Thank God the mission got cancelled. Can't imagine what the French (not to mention the Germans) would have thought had I gotten shot down sporting half a mustache. They would have thought that I was some kind of a clown!

I had completed eight missions by then, but couldn't even remember them all. But I do remember the camaraderie of being with nine other guys. That helped alleviate the fear. At least we're all in this together, I remember thinking. The guys I felt sorry for were the fighter pilots in those little planes, because they were all by themselves.

We, on the other hand, had each other. We were too busy to be scared as we maneuvered this 60,000 pound war bird 25,000 feet above the enemy; coasting along at an estimated indicated speed of150 mph - ready to point out positions of the FW-190s and the ME-109s - that were circling around us like buzzards.

This madness wouldn't last forever, I remember thinking. Twenty-five missions and I'm out of here. Yeah, right! Odds of that happening were about one in four. Ten missions was actually a quite a feat.

Preparing for take off was a busy time for co-pilots. We didn't have time to worry, or wonder about our families, or fiancées. I had to make sure all the crew had a parachute. And then there was the checklist time, the start engine time, the taxi time the takeoff time.

Then we had to be in the right order within our squadron. By January 1943 there were seventy planes on a mission. But within a year, the missions grew to include 300, 400 and possibly as many as 500 B-17s.

We had diversionary missions, too. These were designed to fool the enemy fighters and lure them away from the real action.

We had plenty of fighter escorts accompanying us in early 1943. But, unfortunately they were all German!

For my eighth mission, on March 6, 1943, we went to Lorient, France on the Atlantic coast. U.S. supply ships, bound for England, were getting beat to death in the early part of '43. German submarines were sinking them like mad. So part of our effort was to target submarine pens at St. Nazaire and Lorient. On this particular mission we were trying something new. We formed four groups and passed Land's End (the south end of England) on the deck to avoid Nazi radar. Then, out in the Atlantic, we turned toward the mainland and began our climb. The theory, then, was to hit our bombing altitude and our bomb run at roughly the same time. We were to drop our bombs and fly back out into the Atlantic again, descending all the while. Enemy fighters couldn't follow us very far because of their limited fuel. Then we would turn toward England and spread out. This alleviated the need to pump the throttles to stay in formation, which saved tons of fuel. Very important strategy since this was an eight-hour mission. Later on, B-17Gs, had internal wing tip tanks called 'Tokyo tanks' that could provide extended range, but we didn't have them on our B-17Fs.

Everything worked as planned and we successfully bombed Lorient. We left the target area in high-speed descent, spread out, and headed back to England.

Then things got interesting. On my (the co-pilot's) side, a red light started blinking, signifying that we had just forty-five minutes of fuel left. And by the time we spotted the Land's End area, the red light came on solid, meaning we had just twenty minutes worth of fuel left at full throttle. This was really getting interesting-and scary. Everybody was screaming, "We're running out of fuel . . . we're not going to make it." They were right. There was no way we could get back to the base. Not even close. We had to figure out another place to land. If we didn't we'd be ditching in the English Channel, where some of us would surely die.

The group leader came up with an idea. There was an RAF base near Exeter in the southern part of England. He believed we had enough fuel to get there-barely. And we did. Running on fumes, our whole group sat down, one right after the other. Then we had to get off the runway, fast, to keep from getting hit by another B-17. Service vehicles with grappling hooks were there to yank planes that were out of fuel off the runway. We were one of the first planes down and had just enough fuel to taxi to a dispersal area and park. Then we just sat there and watched. Pilots were coming down and cutting other guys off on the final approach. Everybody made it. Nobody had to bail out. It was one of the scariest things I ever saw.

The RAF airman, who parked us, opened the nose door and a whole pile of spent, .50 caliber shells fell all over him. "Sorry about that," we said. Actually, though, it was kind of funny.

We were assigned quarters there at the RAF base, if you could call them that. The bed I got was no more than a hollowed out piece of wood. There were no blankets, or much of anything else for the RAF's unexpected guests. I couldn't go to sleep. I was just too wired from the day's events. We had a close call today.

Little did I know, however, that the worst was yet to come. The next morning, they fueled us and we flew back to base.

6

MY LAST MISSION

On the night of March 7th we went into town and had a few drinks. I turned in early that night with a knot in my stomach. Every time I closed my eyes I saw Doris and heard her voice over and over saying, "Hon, I love you with all my heart and soul. I can't wait for you to come home so I can hold you every night . . ." I missed her more that night than I had in months.

I felt like crap the next morning, but knew I could go back to bed and try and catch up on my sleep. I wasn't scheduled to go on that day's mission and couldn't care less. I needed some R&R. But fate had different plans for me. As I was heading back to bed from the briefing room Riordan yelled, "Hey, Edris, wanna go with Otto Buddenbaum today? His co-pilot is sick and I think you guys would work well together." I'd always heard that you shouldn't EVER volunteer for anything in the service. But I opened my big mouth and said, "What the hell. I'll go." That impulsive decision would change my life forever. My heart sank when I saw the position of our plane. There were three squadrons of six planes each, and our bomber was the number three plane in the number three squadron. The position was called the "Purple Heart Corner." It was the last plane in the last squadron and stuck way out to the left, like a sitting duck. If planes in this position came back at all there were always wounded on board.

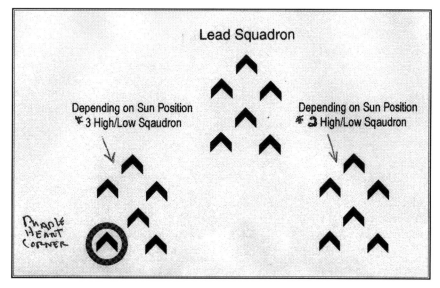

Purple Heart corner formation

23

When we went back to the locker room for parachutes and stuff, I told Riordan that I had a feeling that I wouldn't be coming back. He sloughed off my comment and said, "Don't worry about it, Edris, that's what everybody says."

I didn't know Buddenbaum from Adam. We had never flown together and didn't know crap about our individual flying idiosyncrasies. So we decided that each of us would fly for half an hour. That person would fly the whole thing, throttles and all. We figured that would be the best way to keep from confusing each other. I didn't know the navigator, the gunners, the bombardier . . . I didn't know anybody on this bomber.

Uneventfully, we got the thing off the ground.

If anything goes wrong with the plane before it's half way across the English Channel, we were supposed to turn around and go back. And we had trouble right off the bat. The number two and three engines were not putting out the proper manifold pressure. We were having trouble staying in formation. And when you're stuck out there as the last plane in the last group, you have to pump the throttles all the time to stay in the right place. But we went against our better judgment and decided not to abort.

Because aborted missions often had to go before a humiliating "kangaroo court." The judge would be, by then, General Armstrong, himself. Combat crews would be the jury. And the crews that aborted their missions were almost always "guilty."

Recently a radio operator was out of oxygen and everybody else in the back was throwing up. So . . . that B-17 aborted its mission and returned to base. And sure enough the crew went before the kangaroo court.

The crew was proclaimed "Guilty." And the poor radio operator had to carry a warm bottle of urine in his pocket for days. And show it to anyone who asked.

We decided that we didn't want to be a part of something like that and continued our mission. Stupid reason to continue, but that was the logic you'd expect from twenty-one and twenty-two year old kids.

So we kept going, right across the coast toward our target, Rennes, France, a key marshalling yard for trains.

We were at 25,000 feet and I was flying the plane at the time from the co-pilot's position. We were a little out of formation and I remember I had the wheel down to slide in a bit closer. Then, right out of the blue, three .20 millimeter cannon shells blasted us all at once - one in the right wing, one in the left wing, and one right in the top turret. "Mother, mother," I screamed at the top of my lungs.

At precisely the same moment, back in Manhasset N.Y., Emmabelle Edris bolted out of a deep sleep and cried out, "Oh my God, Junior . . . oh, my God." In the kitchen that morning she put her arms around Pete Edris' sisters, Helen and Lucille, and tearfully said, "Something horrible has happened to Junior. Something horrible . . ."

Then I looked up in sheer terror at the top turret gunner. He was hit in the face and had lost one of his eyes . . . and was bleeding like a stuck pig.

The two blasts to the wings had completely severed the aileron cables (that bank the plane).

Buddenbaum and I both shook the wheel, and there wasn't anything there. Then we started banking, violently. The only way we could straighten was to push the top rudder. It was very hard to push the rudder on a B-17. It became an elevator as it sunk to the left, and then to the right. By now we were out of formation. Way out. Every tail gunner in the group was firing away, trying to help fend off the enemy FW-190s. But we were just too far away. Then engine three caught on fire. Usually when a radial engine catches on fire you only see smoke; you rarely see flames. But this thing had flames coming out the front and coming out under the cowl flaps; and, there was black, thick smoke all the way back as far as I could see.

My drawing of our B-17 after being hit by a FW-190

The fire extinguisher controls were on my side, so I turned the handle for the number three engine and pulled hard. Nothing happened. We had the throttles pushed up as far as they could go, and the one and four engines were over-boosted. Their propeller governors broke and the propellers were going faster and faster. The noise of runaway propellers is like the most horrendous scream you've ever heard.

That's when Buddenbaum himself started screaming, "Bail out, bail out, bail out!"

I quickly ripped off my oxygen mask and screamed back, "No, let's see if we can turn it around and get back to the Channel." But by that time the FW-190 was making another pass. He came in from the rear at 6:00 O'clock high. Nobody saw him coming. (A hit from 6:00 0'clock was unusual. After examining wrecked B-17s and B-24s, Luftwaffe (German air force) officers discovered that it took more shells to bring B-17s down from the rear. They found that B-17s were much more vulnerable at the front, from12:00 0'clock high.

On his second pass he hit our cockpit, as well as the little aisle space between us. The 20mm rounds likely were fused for no delay. That meant they blew up when the nose of the shell hit the skin of the airplane. Our seats were backed by a big 5/8" thick piece of steel armor plate. We used to say they were for morale purposes, but they saved our lives. They literally stopped the shrapnel. But there was nothing to stop the shrapnel that hit between us. It knocked out most of the instruments and destroyed all the throttle handles.

It even knocked out the little window above my head, which crashed down and bloodied my knee.

Up in the top turret the gunner was jammed in and trying to fight his way out. Finally, he freed himself and ended up in the aisle, right between Buddenbaum and me. He was bleeding profusely from where his eye used to be. I didn't understand why he hadn't bled to death. Blood was spurting all over us and onto the windshield.

After the second pass of the FW-190, Buddenbaum and I were hopelessly still fighting with the plane.

Meanwhile, the German fighter came up and flew formation on our right wing . . . right beside of me. Guess he was trying to see what was holding us up. If I'd had a shoulder holster with a .45 caliber in it, I could've opened the window and blown his brains out. He peeled off and I thought, "Oh my God, we're going to get it again."

After his third pass, I said, "That's enough!" I jumped out of my seat and got stuck between the seats. Buddenbaum hit my chute with his fist, trying to push me through. I finally fell through, down onto the catwalk. Below, I found the bombardier and the navigator fighting with the nose door that wouldn't jettison. This door has a red handle attached by cables to the two hinge pins. When you pull the handle it pulls the pins out and the door falls off. The navigator pulled the handle but the cables broke, so the door was flapping in the slipstream. I said, "Get the hell out!"

(Everyone but Buddenbaum had bailed out. He was still up there fighting to control the plane; and fighting a losing battle).

The bombardier held the door for the navigator, and I held the door for the bombardier. But there was no one to hold the door for me.

So I'm pushing hard against that door. I've got my head and shoulder against it, trying to pry it open enough to get out. I've got these straps from the parachute harness and I'm pushing hard, trying to jump out. And hoping and praying that my harness doesn't get caught on the big, inside door handle, tethering me to a 60,000 -pound Molotov cocktail, spinning toward a fiery hell.

Luckily, it didn't.

I remembered reading a book about how to bail out. It said, "If you're tumbling, spread eagle; arms and legs, and you'll stop tumbling." When I went out I was tumbling a mile a minute. And if you open up your chute in the wrong position, the chute can come up right between your legs. Then you'll flip and could literally break your back.

So here I was, tumbling away. I went spread eagle like the book said, but not with both hands. I didn't take my hand off the ripcord because of a story I never forgot. Some pilot in the thirties had to bail out of a military plane. He had a leather jacket on, and in his panic he got confused and thought the ripcord was on the wrong side. They found him in the field with his leather jacket torn and his skin bloodied from where he tried to get at the ripcord from the wrong side.

So when I was spread eagle, I kept my hand on the ripcord. After a couple of seconds, the tumbling stopped. I was in a facedown position when the chute opened and it did a number on my back. When it opened it jerked me straight up. It opened beautifully, but I was going horizontal, like a swing. Every time I went horizontal, one half of the chute collapsed. I tried arching my back trying to stop the swing. Finally, I was so exhausted, that I just hung there.

The whole trip down took about thirty minutes. In a twenty-four foot in diameter chute with a normal weight, you fall at eleven feet per second. You actually slow down if you are free falling. If you free fall at 25,000 feet, you fall at 175 miles per hour. If you fell all the way to the ground without opening your chute, you'd hit the ground going about 125 miles mph because of the increased density in the air.

And it was colder than you can imagine; about forty degrees below zero. When the chute opened my escape kit tore out of my zippered knee pocket. The escape kit had silk maps, morphine, a syringe, d-bar (chocolate, 600 calories), compass and file. Have no idea what the hell the file was for. Did the Army think we were going to saw our way out of some jail? The kit was in two pieces. The other piece was a rubberized container, containing seventy-five francs. It stayed stuck in my pocket.

On the way down I lost the boot and shoe from my right foot. Then I took the boot off my left shoe and put it on my right foot. Not for the cold-I didn't' really notice the cold that much. I just didn't want to land on the ground without something to protect my right foot.

Thirty minutes is a lot of time. And I didn't have anything better to do.

Then I realized that I had my wallet. It's the first time I had been on a mission without leaving my wallet behind. Wallets can contain incriminating stuff that the Germans can use. So I went to work cleaning it out. I tore up my driver's license, I.D. cards and anything else that could help the Germans. I tore up everything but Doris' picture and nine pounds of British money. Never knew when I might need it, but no time soon I was sure.

Overall, my bailout was pretty uneventful. While I was falling, I tried to look back and watch the airplane. The last I remember it was going down in a circle. Buddenbaum, I feared, never got out. I was also worried that the bomber might end up killing a bunch of innocent French people.

Thank God, I remember thinking: I didn't get tangled up in that door handle.

I had my own theory about landing with a parachute. There's a strap above you on each side. I thought that if you reached up and grabbed the straps and pulled down, you could get a cushioning effect. The last 500 feet were coming on fast, like they were being thrown up toward me. I was looking down and just as I thought I was going to hit, I pulled on those two straps. I put my right foot in the air. When I landed on my left foot, my knee bent and I just stood there and put my right food down on the ground. I had actually made a standing landing.

I sat down and started shaking like a leaf. I couldn't stop trembling. The whole ordeal was hitting me like a ton of bricks. I was in a daze. Everything was surreal. Then I saw people running toward me. I threw my empty wallet away and a little kid retrieved it and brought it back. I made a point to save the ripcord. There's an old saying in the States that if you bail out, and you don't bring your ripcord back to the Officers' Club, the drinks are on you. I must have been delusional. Why would I be thinking about something so trivial as having to buy drinks at the Officer's Club!

I dug out four Chesterfield cigarettes and almost ate one. I gave the other three to the Frenchmen who had come to my aid.

I was dying of thirst but I couldn't remember the word for water in French, so I just made some motions, opening my mouth and pointing to my throat.

Leave it the French! They didn't bring me water; they brought me wine in a big jug; homemade for sure.

It wasn't exactly a thirst quencher, but I turned up the jug and chugged it down, nonetheless.

Wine never tasted so good.

7

ON THE RUN

One of the Frenchmen yelled, "Allamande, Allamande! German, German!" Everybody except one Frenchman ran off and left me. This fellow quickly grabbed my arms and led me to a pigsty. So there I was, a Yankee from New Jersey in a muddy, stinking pigsty. I didn't know anything about pigs. They ate people as far as I knew. They were huge and grunting and wondering what the hell I was doing in there. I'd never seen a pig before. The nearest I'd ever been to a pig was a ham and cheese sandwich back in high school.

My first "safe haven" was this pig sty near Lamballe, France

A German truck was circling all around. I could hear the Germans outside interviewing the French people. They did very little searching. They didn't even think about looking inside the pigsty. Soon they gave up and I heard the German trucks roaring off. Once they were gone my new French friends quickly put me inside an empty chicken coop for the rest of the day.

This place wasn't nearly as bad as the pigsty. At least it was dry and the straw there served as a nice cushion for my exhausted body. I just sat there, wondering what in the world would happen next.

A nice woman came by and gave me some bread, wine and a hard-boiled egg. I would have loved some water, but the French water was contaminated and not fit for human consumption. That's why they drank so much wine. After I finished eating, the woman came back and covered her tracks, and my presence, by picking up all the eggshells. That was my first lesson on evasion. Then she asked me to follow her back to the farmhouse. She led me into a room that was filled with people; men, women and children. Then she asked me to undress, right there in front of everybody. She handed me a stack of fresh, clean clothes including a sweater, a pair of pants, and some slippers.

That night a guy, wearing a business suit, came along and introduced himself as Henri Du Fretay. He was from St. Brieux, a tiny village about thirteen miles away, on Highway 368, on the northwestern tip of France. He told me we were near Lamballe and that he wanted to escort me up to St. Brieux - by foot, of course.

That's when I realized that the slippers didn't fit very well, which later led to the loss of an entire toenail. Painful was not the word for it. We walked and walked and I remembered the French word for sleep was "dormir," and that's what I told Monsieur Du Fretay that I was in desperate need of. He listened.

A little later we stopped at a farmhouse and were let in by a guy who obviously knew Monsieur Du Fretay. He fed us a potato stew of some sort that we dipped up with big hunks of white bread torn from a huge loaf. We also drank some homemade red wine.

Then we left and continued our walk. Around dawn Du Fretay flagged down a truck and got us a ride to St. Brieux, about five miles up the road.

There, Monsieur Du Fretay led me off the beaten path to another "safe house" and took me in through the front door. Waiting for us was a nervous French woman, who quickly led me upstairs into a small bedroom. I slept like a baby all day.

Farmhouse near St. Brieux, France where I had a "feast" of potato soup

That night, Monsieur Du Fretay came for me and we walked across the street to my next hideout. This was the home of Madame Dinten and her lovely daughter, Janelou. These people were angels. They knew what they were doing. I knew right away that I probably wasn't the first shot down American airman that they had hidden from the Germans. The first thing Madame Dinten did was lead me up into the attic. I felt safe up there, for sure. But I was also hungry and very sore. I was aching from head to toe. When I complained about my pain Madame Dinten seemed to understand my English. After a meal of veal, rice and hot potato soup, Madame Dinten gave me a back rub, which she repeated a couple of times a day for the three days I was there. After a hot bath on that first night, I discovered blood marks from the parachute straps around my thighs and in the groin area. I also had crimson red marks all over my shoulders from the shoulder straps. I was a mess.

And it got worse.

I discovered that the sweater I was given back at the farmhouse in Lamballe was infested with fleas. I had flea -bites all over my chest and back and arms. They were driving me crazy!

But sweet Madame Dinten came to the rescue and washed the sweater, three times. I got the feeling that this was not the first flea-infested sweater that Madame Dinten had encountered.

At the end of my three- day stay at Madame Dinten's, a fellow by the name of Eric DelVal, who was a doctor, showed up at the house. Eric was the next spoke in my wheel of evasion. These people were literally risking their lives for me. I don't know where Eric came from, but his mission was clear: Keep me on the move . . . and out of harm's way. People like Eric Del Val, Madame Dinten and Monsieur Du Fretay were among the thousands of unsung heroes who harbored American and allied soldiers in occupied Europe during World War II.

Eric Dulval, Madame Dinten and Monsieru Corbel

Eric must have lived very near to Madame Dinten because he showed up with two bicycles. He advised me that we should stay on the move because it wasn't safe to stay at any one place more than two or three days. Our next stop, he said, was a little town called Longidias, about a six- hour bike ride north.

This was a nerve-wracking trip. We rode through the middle of small country towns that were brimming with German soldiers. When they saw us coming they would step back out of the way, although as far as I knew, bikes didn't have the right of way. I tried to look like just a regular, carefree Frenchman, but I felt as if the Germans were staring at me. "Just your imagination," Eric said.

He did devise a signal, though. He was wearing a scarf around his neck that he would remove when he saw Germans. That was his sign for me to ride at least a hundred feet behind him. He thought it was less conspicuous if it appeared that we were traveling separately.

When he thought it was safe for us to ride together, he would put the scarf back on. He repeated this scarf "exercise" several times during the trip. He was particularly concerned when alert and nosey German Shepherds accompanied the Germans. Those were the guys who were the most serious about capturing shot down airmen, Eric thought.

Ironically, one of my tires blew out right as we were getting into Longidias. If this had happened a mile or two back, it would have drawn a lot of attention from the Germans, and I probably would have been captured.

In the heart of Longidias was the house of the parish priest, Monsieur L' Abbé. Corbel. It was to be my next "safe haven."

Monsieur Corbel's maid, Mary, greeted us at the door and invited us in. Monsieur Corbel greeted us with a huge smile, a warm handshake and then a big hug. That evening after dinner he left for a few minutes and returned with a bottle of cognac. It was dusty and covered with cobwebs and was housed in a straw container.

He said, "I was saving this for the liberation, but to me this occasion is special too. Welcome to my home, Lieutenant Edris!"

Monsieur Corbel with his maid

He told me I would be there about two weeks, longer than the usual stay for an airman on the run. "But the Germans have left me alone up to now, so I'm not expecting any trouble. I think you'll be safe here for these two weeks, lieutenant."

They grew vegetables in the farm area behind the house and I ate pretty well while I was there. There was no indoor plumbing, however, so I used a chamber pot that was under my bed.

It was dreadfully cold in my bedroom so Mary brought up a hot water bottle every night. Although Monsieur Corbel believed I would be safe there, I couldn't help but worry. I was almost in a cold sweat the whole time I was there. What was going on back home I wondered? And for some reason that night I couldn't get my mind off my mother . . .

WESTERN UNION

**MARCH 15, 1943
MRS EMMABELLE K EDRIS
127 KNICKERBOCKER RD MANHASSET NY**

THE SECRETARY OF WAR DESIRES ME TO EXPRESS HIS DEEP REGRET THAT YOUR SON FIRST LIEUTENANT WARREN P EDRIS HAS BEEN REPORTED MISSING IN ACTION SINCE EIGHT MARCH PERIOD ADDITIONAL INFORMATION WILL BE SENT YOU WHEN RECEIVED . . .

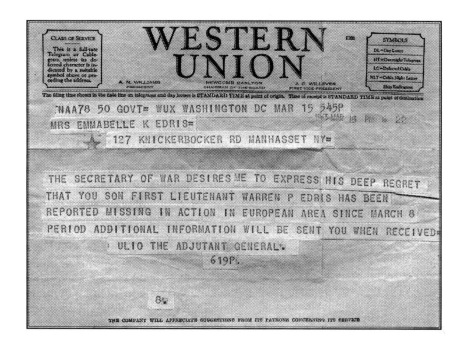

Manhasset Mail, Thursday, March 25, 1943

Lt. W. P. Edris Reported Missing

Mrs. W. P. Edris, 127 Knickerbocker road, has been notified by the War Department, in a telegraph signed by Adjutant General Ulio, that her son, First Lieutenant War-

1st Lieut. Edris

ren Peter Edris Jr., has been missing in European action since March 8. Lt. Edris, stationed in England, piloted a Flying Fortress.

He graduated from Oak Ridge Military Institute Junior College, enlisted in 1941, received his wings at Kay Field, and in April was promoted to the rank of first lieutenant.

The young officer's mother is treasurer of the Strathmore Vanderbilt Red Cross Workroom, serves as an Air Raid Warden for Knickerbocker road, and is a member of the Daughters of the American Revolution.

Mrs. Edris has another son, Robert B. Edris, who is in Officers Training School, Camp Croft, S. C.

My two weeks went by uneventfully with Monsieur Corbel and it was time to move on. My next guide was another priest, Monsieur L' Abbé Barre. He got my bicycle tire fixed and we headed off to a town called Dinan, a well-preserved, walled medieval town in Northeast Brittany.

It was about a two or three- hour bike ride and we saw very few Germans along the way. (Thankfully, none of them were accompanied by dogs). A family, who wouldn't give us their names, put us up there and fed us. They wouldn't let us spend but one night there because they were terrified. They feared the Germans would be knocking on their door at any minute and they feared for their lives. I felt really sorry for them. Everything worked out, though,

My next guide was a black man of Haitian descent, Jacques Coicou, who arrived from Paris with his apartment building janitor, a Spaniard. Coicou was an affable guy and a medical doctor. He was stranded in Paris because of the war and was married to a white French girl, Suzanne. Interracial marriage wasn't unusual in France.

Jacques and his janitor and I headed off by foot to the train station in Dinan as the unnamed family nervously waved goodbye.

On the train there were four or five other people in our compartment. Jacques quickly realized that one of the women in there was German and promptly took me out into the hallway. The narrow hallway was on one side of the train, opposite the small compartments.

"Lieutenant," he said, "Remember . . . you are deaf and dumb and I'm taking you to Paris for an operation to restore your hearing. I know this will be hard for you, since you're such a talkative guy, but you've got to keep your mouth shut. Period."

This was going to be tough. I had never gone very long without talking. Much less for the ten hours that this train ride to Paris was going to take.

I had a pass from the Prefect (Chief) of Police of Paris who was a friend of Jacques.' The Prefect was more or less a double agent, who helped me while at the same time cooperating with the Germans. My cover name was Dombrosky, and I was a Czech slave laborer being taken to Paris for an operation.

After enduring the longest ten hours of my life, we finally arrived in Paris. And I could talk again. We soon boarded the propaganda- filled subway. There were posters everywhere depicting Roosevelt and Churchill as devils. The Germans were even depicting Roosevelt as a Jew. Our destination was #1 Rue de Lord Byron, the site of Jacque and Suzanne's apartment building. Suzanne was an attractive woman and she greeted me very warmly. Their plan was for me to stay there for six weeks. "A little long, don't you think?" I asked Jacques. He said, "Yes, I know. But if you get caught, it's my neck, too."

He was helping me on his own. He was not a member of the underground, an "organization" that the Germans never tried to break up. They actually fed it with counter espionage; mainly French turncoats or Germans acting like French. These turncoats would then turn members of the underground over to the Gestapo in Paris.

I still had my seventy-five francs and Jacques had them changed into pesos. Our plan was to take the train to Bordeaux in the south of France and pick up guides who would take me across the Pyrenees to Spain; then to Portugal. While crossing the Pyrenees, the object was not to say anything to anybody. Keep your identity entirely to yourself until you could get to an American embassy. After all, this was Franco's Spain; a Spain that sided with the Nazis. Too many downed airmen didn't realize that fact, and ended up spending many months in Spanish prisons.

But for me to get all the way to Portugal, I would need help from the underground; my six weeks with Jacques and Suzanne were about up. Finally, Jacques found someone who could help me. Her name was Madam Feldon, an American woman who had been, like Jacques, stuck in France because of the war.

Jacques said she would be at the apartment after dark that night.

Jacques' and Suzanne's apartment was on the fifth floor of a five story building. There was even a door that opened up to the flat roof. The day of Madam Feldon's visit I sat up there and watched the skies light up to the west. A group of B-17s was bombing a factory that made Renault automobiles (probably because they weren't making cars, but German tanks). It was quite a scene . . . quite a light show.

That night, about 9, Madame Feldon knocked on the door and Suzanne led her into the living room where I sat, smoking a cigarette. The first thing I noticed about Madam Feldon was that she was very pregnant. She was also very nice and seemed sincerely interested in me, and my plight. "How long have you been in France?" she asked. "Well," I said, "Ever since I was shot down on March 8th".

"It's already the middle of May, lieutenant," said Madam Feldon. "You're pushing your luck . . . especially here in Paris. The Gestapo is all over the place. We need to get you out of here. My plan is to get you back to the Brittany Peninsula, where you'll board a Lysander monoplane, bound for England.

"Uh . . . would you like to take some military information with you?"

"Well sure, I guess so," I said. "But not anything in writing. Just feed me the information and I'll memorize it."

She proceeded to tell me how the Germans got some submarines from Germany to St. Nazarre by train, in pieces. Then they would assemble them there on the coast. I'm not sure this was true but she seemed to know what she was talking about. Then she gave me information about the extent of the bomb damage at Rennes, the site to which I was headed when I was shot down. She said she could walk freely around Paris because nobody would mess with a woman who was eight months pregnant. She promised to finalize her plans on getting me out . . . and would return for me "in a few days." Hopefully, she won't go into labor first, I was thinking to myself.

8

MORNING OF THE GESTAPO

A couple of days later, on May 15, 1943, I was killing time, looking through some of Jacques' medical books in his office. Jacques was sitting at his desk, going through some papers. We were having a very quiet and peaceful morning. Then all hell broke loose. A thunderous bang brought the door off its hinges and in strutted a swastika- adorned member of Hitler's Gestapo. He was a tall blond haired, blue-eyed Aryan. And he meant business. I was scared stiff. And Jacques, who was as black as you can get, had literally turned a weird shade of gray. The German looked at Jacques and said, "Votre papier, monsieur," (Your papers, sir!) Then he looked at me and said, "Et vous?" Not trusting my French, I just shrugged my shoulders. Then he said, in perfect English, "You are an American flying officer, aren't you?" I just shrugged again. Then he just jerked me around and slammed on the handcuffs. He pulled out another set of cuffs and said, "You too, monsieur." "Okay, come with me," he said. "Let's get the women and get out of here." So Jacques and me, and Susanne and the maid were pushed onto the elevator. Awaiting us on the street was a van with little cells on each side of an isle. Each cell had a little seat/ledge, and there were bars on the windows. It was a little prison on wheels. And the siren blared, "Bee baa, Bee baa." The sound was piercing and almost nauseating. This thing wailed all the way to Fresnes Prison, just south of Paris. The sounds of sirens have haunted me ever since.

I don't know what they did with Suzanne and the maid because that was the last I saw of them. Jacques and I were led together through the gate and into a sentry area. I was so afraid . . . what were they going to do next? Were they going to kill Jacques and Suzanne . . . and the maid?

I was marched off through an underground tunnel to a room with a dirt floor. No doubt, we were in the midst of the Gestapo. Four or five other people, one of whom was a priest, occupied the little room. A Gestapo brat was making all of us strip so he could inspect our bodies. I remember the priest saying (with hand signs) "Me too? After all, I'm a priest." Finally the kid shook his head and said the equivalent of "Okay." I walked up to this kid, tapped him on the shoulder, and told him I was an American officer, POW. The minute I touched him he recoiled and glared at me like I was a leper.

That first day around noon I was given a piece of bread, and a bowl of soup, and that was it. I didn't even eat it. I was really scared. Being in prison felt weird. I thought about my mother. And I thought about Doris and how much I missed her. I wondered what she was doing. What I would have given to be with her, holding her in my arms . . . and never letting go. I had never felt so lonely in my whole life, or miserable either.

The next day they moved me from the first floor to the third floor. Fresnes prison was just like you saw in the movies. There were catwalks and cells along either side and a "well" in the center four floors high. The cells had thick, wooden doors each with a tiny peephole and a sliding brass plate on the outside. There was one light bulb per cell, which was controlled from the outside.

They kept me in solitary confinement for seventy-seven days. I had a table and a chair. The chair was chained to the wall (So I couldn't use it to hit somebody over the head, I supposed). There was a cot. And a commode with no seat or lid. A faucet came out of the wall that had a push button for flushing the toilet. My button didn't work. They brought me a pail of water every morning for drinking, flushing, and washing. But that was it. There was no soap, nor washcloth. No towel. No toothbrush . . . no comb.

My little cell was about twelve feet long by five or six feet wide. I had one window, but it was frosted so you couldn't see out. Except mine had a little crack in it and a small piece of glass had actually broken out, allowing me a view, of sorts. I could peek through and look out at a hill. I could see people out there planting vegetables. I followed the gardens' growth week after week. It was my only connection to the outside world.

We got what they called coffee every morning. But actually it wasn't coffee at all-it was ersatz coffee made from burnt acorns.

They gave me a little pan that was about three inches deep and around eight inches in diameter.

The bread at Fresnes was black and tough. I got one big hunk a day, about four by six inches big.

They brought the bread at noon along with soup. I'd go to the door with my pan where a guard and a French prisoner, pushing a tureen, awaited me. He would dip into the tureen and dump the soup into my pan. Although they called it vegetable soup, it was little more than potatoes and water, although a tree leaf or two popped up every now and then.

What I noticed most, though, were the bugs and worms. The bugs were tiny and round and the worms were about an inch long. I'd scoop them out with my spoon and pick them out with my fingers, and wipe them on my pants. I'm sure I ended up eating a few, too. But I had no choice except to eat this stuff. It was my only meal of the day. And it was about the only activity I had.

We weren't allowed to lie down until bedtime. Sheer boredom wasn't the word for it.

My only diversion was the "book mobile." About three or four times during my seventy-seven days in solitary a guy came by pushing a book cart. But my asshole guard would give me only a few seconds to pick something out. Not much time when you need something in English.

But I remember once finding "The Mortal Storm." There was actually a movie adapted from this book before we entered the war. It's a story about French people escaping over the Alps from the Gestapo. The guards didn't have a clue that this book was in the prison.

In the margins guys had pressed words into the paper, probably using their spoon handles. Things like, "Keep your chin up" and "Have faith" and other inspirational words were spread throughout the book. What a great morale builder hearing from other prisoners and knowing I wasn't there alone. No doubt, "misery loves company."

I read "The Mortal Storm" over and over, every word. I probably read it three or four times before the book cart guy finally came to pick it up.

The book gave me some solace and respite from the verbal abuse I was encountering.

My guard was ruthless. He once said, "Vous etes un sabateur." You are a spy, a saboteur and you are going to be shot." He made it clear that I was going to be executed and I had no reason whatsoever not to believe him. I would say: "I'm an American officer and you can't treat me this way. He would say: "Who the hell are you? You're just a pebble on the beach. They're killing people all over the world. Nobody's going to miss you."

He had the key. He had the gun. And he always had the last word.

One day I heard a voice ask, "Can anybody hear me out there?" I hollered out my little window, "Yeah, me!" He said, "My name is Larsen and I'm on the first floor."

"Well, I'm Pete Edris," I yelled. "And I'm on the third floor of this dump."

Larsen had been there only a month or so, he said. He had a good sense of humor and helped keep my morale up.

One day he yelled, "Edris, you know if it wasn't for the worms in the soup we'd all starve to death!"

That was the day the guard caught me hollering at Larsen and got all pissed off. He took his bare hand and slapped me up side the head several times. And all I could do was stand there and take it.

When he left he inadvertently left the peephole open and I took advantage by peering through it. I could see the guard on the other side sneaking from cell to cell without making a sound. No wonder he wasn't making a sound. No wonder I didn't hear his footsteps earlier that day. His feet were covered with straw. What a sneak!

And what a jerk, too! Sometimes he would turn on my light in the middle of the night, just to annoy me.

But fleas had become my biggest annoyance. They were everywhere. My cot was loaded with fleas. My belt kept the fleas away from my upper body, but I was a mess from the waist down. One day I counted over 500 fleabites below the belt. I was allergic to the bites and they swelled up as large as my little fingernail. I scratched so much that they became infected. One day I yelled and pleaded for medical treatment. The answer I got was, "You're a spy and you're going to be executed."

I had never been more lonely and depressed . . . and scared. I was cooped up in this tiny little room, sweating and itching from the fleabites and wondering if I was going to die and rot in here. If there was such a thing as hell on earth I had a ringside seat. I wanted to scream but what good would it do. God, I felt, had truly forsaken me. And my mother and my dearest Doris . . . they must be worried sick.

WESTERN UNION

NP 53 GOVT=WUX WASHINGTON DC JULY 11 100 4A 1943
MRS EMMABELLE K EDRIS=
127 KNICKERBOCKER RD MANHASSETT NY=

REPORT RECEIVED FROM THE GERMAN GOVERNMENT THROUGH THE INTERNATIONAL RED CROSS STATES THAT YOUR SON FIRST LIEUTENANT WARREN P EDRIS WHO WAS PREVIOUSLY REPORTED MISSING SINCE EIGHT MARCH WAS KILLED IN ACTION ON EIGHT MARCH IN THE EUROPEAN AREA THE SECRETARY OF WAR SHARES YOUR GRIEF AND EXTENDS HIS DEEP SYMPATHY LETTER FOLLOWS=ULIO THE ADJUTANT GENERAL

This telegram was delivered in person to Emmabelle Edris. She read it and stood there dazed . . . and in shock.

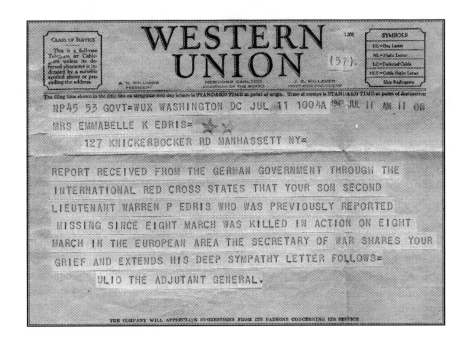

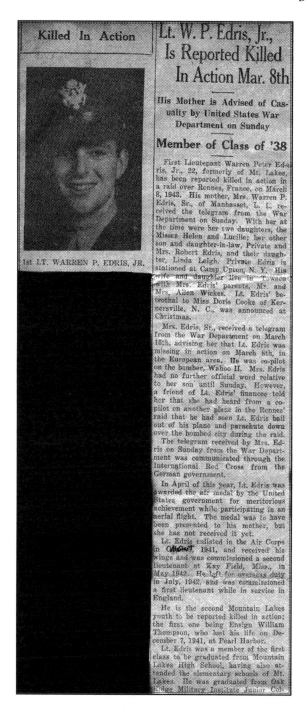

Killed In Action

Lt. W. P. Edris, Jr., Is Reported Killed In Action Mar. 8th

His Mother is Advised of Casualty by United States War Department on Sunday

Member of Class of '38

First Lieutenant Warren Peter Edris, Jr., 22, formerly of Mt. Lakes, has been reported killed in action in a raid over Rennes, France, on March 8, 1943. His mother, Mrs. Warren P. Edris, Sr., of Manhasset, L. I., received the telegram from the War Department on Sunday. With her at the time were her two daughters, the Misses Helen and Lucille; her other son and daughter-in-law, Private and Mrs. Robert Edris, and their daughter, Linda Leigh. Private Edris is stationed at Camp Upton, N. Y. His wife and daughter live in Owaco with Mrs. Edris' parents, Mr. and Mrs. Allen Wickes. Lt. Edris' betrothal to Miss Doris Cooke of Kernersville, N. C., was announced at Christmas.

Mrs. Edris, Sr., received a telegram from the War Department on March 15th, advising her that Lt. Edris was missing in action on March 8th, in the European area. He was co-pilot on the bomber, Wahoo II. Mrs. Edris had no further official word relative to her son until Sunday. However, a friend of Lt. Edris' fiancee told her that she had heard from a co-pilot on another plane in the Rennes' raid that he had seen Lt. Edris bail out of his plane and parachute down over the bombed city during the raid. The telegram received by Mrs. Edris on Sunday from the War Department was communicated through the International Red Cross from the German government.

In April of this year, Lt. Edris was awarded the air medal by the United States government for meritorious achievement while participating in an aerial flight. The medal was to have been presented to his mother, but she has not received it yet.

Lt. Edris enlisted in the Air Corps in August 1941, and received his wings and was commissioned a second lieutenant at Kay Field, Miss., in May 1942. He left for overseas duty in July, 1942, and was commissioned a first lieutenant while in service in England.

He is the second Mountain Lakes youth to be reported killed in action; the first one being Ensign William Thompson, who lost his life on December 7, 1941, at Pearl Harbor.

Lt. Edris was a member of the first class to be graduated from Mountain Lakes High School, having also attended the elementary schools of Mt. Lakes. He was graduated from Oak Ridge Military Institute Junior Col-

1st LT. WARREN P. EDRIS, JR.

July 23, 1943

My Dear Doris

Well dear, all our hopes and plans are gone, and I feel so heartbroken, it seems as if I just can't go on-

Yesterday I received a letter from the War Department confirming their telegram - they say Junior died while on an operational mission over Lamballe, France, in the European Area. I don't know just where that is, but will look it up some day. I rather think it is near Rennes. The information came from Germany through the International Red Cross.

I just can't believe I'll never see him again and to lose one of my children in such a way is just awful. If the enemy machine gunned his parachute and he died quickly, that would be some relief, but if he had to suffer long-well I could at this moment kill someone myself. He was so fine and so young and had such hopes for the future - it just isn't fair.

That he met and knew and loved you dear, for that I am glad-and that he knew all about your ring – he did live long enough for that happiness, and he was so proud of you.

I can't say much to you dear, my heart is too full. All we have now are memories. I just can't believe it – and I am bitter. I shouldn't be but I am.

I'll send a clipping to you from our Mountain Lakes paper – I can not write more. God bless you dear for all you meant to him and don't forget us all here. Helen and Lucille send their love.

Lovingly yours,

Pete's Mother

One day I heard a tap, tap, tap coming from the cell next door. Then the taps became uneven, with breaks between. Then I figured out what was going on. This guy was trying to send Morse code to me by tapping with his spoon. But how do you do dashes and dots by tapping on the wall? I finally figured it out: One dot was an "a," two dots was a "b," three dots was a "c" and so on. We learned to abbreviate like mad using this system, but it was still very tedious. But we sure as hell didn't have anything better to do.

That is until the German priest gave me a surprise visit. The first thing I did was grab his arm and say, "You've got to get me out of here!"

He said, "Son, I can't help you, but I can give you something to read." He gave me the Gospel According to St. Matthew. Sadly, I lost that book somewhere, or else it would be on the mantle, framed in gold. It was a little book, no more than three by four inches, and I read it over and over. I practically memorized it.

The priest also gave me a prayer, but I didn't even look at it until after he left. And then my mouth fell open. Right at the top were the words: "Prepare to Meet Your Maker."

I almost threw up. Maybe the guard has been telling the truth. Maybe they *are* going to execute me. I tore up the prayer and threw it in the commode.

The next day I heard tapping from next door that said the Germans had invaded Syracuse. I thought, "My God, they've made it to upstate New York?" My next door neighbor explained by tapping Syracuse, Sicily.

The guy next door told me that they were letting him go home because his wound wouldn't heal. He asked the guard for permission to visit me before he left. The guard granted his wish. On rare occasions the guard could actually be decent. He even gave me a cigarette one day.

Anyhow, he let the guy in to see me. I had learned through our "tapping" system that his name was Francel and he was a Frenchman who spoke English. He had a severe bullet injury that wasn't healing and the Germans were letting him go home. We spent a few moments together and wished each other luck. As he was leaving he said, "Oh, I almost forgot to give you this." He handed me his toothbrush.

I don't remember the last time I brushed my teeth, so I brushed and brushed. And they bled like mad.

Before, when I ran my tongue over my teeth they felt almost slimy dirty.

I had been praying a lot since I read St. Matthew's Gospel over and over. The only prayer I knew was the Lord's Prayer and I prayed it over and over. After finishing it one morning I looked up and said, "God, if you don't get me out of here to hell with you!"

I was at my wit's end. I was desperate. And I was blaming God. "What next, God," I asked. "What next?"

The answer to "what next" came the next day. They came and took me away for interrogation. Larson, down on the first floor, had warned me about what and what not to do. "Don't give them your name, rank, serial number or anything," he said. "You aren't in the military now. They don't care about military crap. All they care about is who helped you. Make up a story and stick to it over and over. Make it as truthful as possible without giving away names of people or places."

And that's exactly what I did. I told myself the story over and over. I looked for loopholes, continually refining my story. I didn't want to have to say, "I can't tell you that."

They took me into Paris, to Gestapo headquarters. It was a big, long gray stone building with the entrance in the middle. They took me into an office that had a full-length mirror where I had to look at myself. I had this scraggly beard. I looked emaciated. I was filthy. If you met me in a dark alley you'd turn and run the other way.

My interrogator seemed a bit addled and maybe not very experienced. To cover up his insecurity he bragged a lot about himself, saying such things as he could speak five languages. He interrogated me for four hours. He asked me questions and then I would fire a question back. One question I asked was what will they do to Jacques, Suzanne and their maid? He made no bones about it. "They will be shot," he exclaimed. My heart sank. I felt the life go out of me.

Then I got defensive and turned into a smartass. That provoked the interrogator to start smacking me around. Then he started bragging about German victories. "We knocked out ninety Russian tanks yesterday," he said. And then I said, "There will be ninety more American ones there tomorrow." That's when he really hit me. And that one hurt.

Then he put a map of France on a large table in the middle of the office. He asked me where I was shot down. I drew a circle around all of France and said, "It was somewhere in there." Then he hit me again. I said, "I'm just a chauffeur. Pilots don't know where the hell we're going. Talk to the navigator. He's the guy who knows where we're going."

This was no fun, but at least I was getting the feeling that they weren't going to shoot me. Next he asked about being shot down. "What happened after you hit the ground?"

"Well, as soon as I hit the ground some French people came to help me."

"What were their names?"

"I don't know. I didn't ask them their names. Would you have asked for their names?"

He paused and said, "Probably not. Uh, what happened next?"

I said, "We walked all night." And I told him the whole story. He kept wanting to know the names of towns and people. And I kept saying I had no idea. He finally accepted the fact that he wasn't going to get this information.

He must have been getting hungry, too, because he pulled out a bag with a sandwich in it. I stared at the sandwich. Then he looked at me and asked, "You did have breakfast, didn't you?"

"You know damn well I haven't eaten anything," I snapped. Then he actually tore the sandwich in two and gave me half. Then he gave me a cigarette. It had been a while since I'd smoked and I inhaled it hard and almost passed out.

For four hours we'd sat there and yakked back and forth. Finally, he said, "We're going to put you in the military section of the prison."

Finally done, they hauled me back to the fourth floor at Fresnes. That night I got a "real" dinner of mashed potatoes, meat and a vegetable!

In a couple of days they said I would be going to a prisoner of war camp in Germany. In the meantime I was going to a cell down on the first floor. Four other airmen were already in there. It was obvious they'd just been caught because they still had their uniforms on. Since I had been in solitary for seventy-seven days, it was a joy just to be with other guys. I couldn't stop talking. They couldn't either. Finally, a guard had had enough. He came in and told us to shut up.

When our two days were up they came and marched us out to a bus bound for Gare du Norde train station in Paris.

There, alongside the trains, we walked single file, accompanied by guards carrying machine guns.

We could see French people out of sight of the guards, holding up their hands in a "V" for victory. It was crowded with a lot of civilian traffic. People were milling about everywhere. Since I was in civilian clothes, it crossed my mind to roll under the train, come out on the other side, and blend in with the crowd.

If I got caught, though, they'd haul me back to Fresnes and into solitary confinement. If they didn't shoot me first!

9

ON MY WAY TO BECOMING A POW

We boarded the train at Gare du Norde bound for Frankfurt in West Germany, the site of Du Lag Luft. This was a transient camp that was used to prepare prisoners for their permanent camps. The Luftwaffe interrogated me there. This was military grilling all the way: name, rank and serial number. There was an American there who belonged to the German American Bund, a radical right wing group who was sympathetic to Hitler and his National Socialist Party. They were very active in the States and had conventions all over the country. When I gave my address this guy said, "So you're from New Jersey." I said, "Yes," and he said, "Well . . . I've been to Mountain Lakes. I was connected with a German American Bund just down the road on Route 6."

The Luftwaffe major then jumped in and asked me what a YB40 was.

I told him I didn't know. "Look, I've been here since March and I have no idea what a YB40 is."

But I did know. It was a B-17 that was more or less a flying battleship. It was loaded with guns. There were about eighteen guns on those planes all fully loaded with ammunition. There were no bombs on the YB40. Instead, the bomb bay was filled with extra fuel tanks. A classmate of mine flew on them and was not impressed. The extra fuel made them too heavy to fly, he said.

"I see you were in the 306th Bomb Group, 369th Bomb Squad," said the major. "And you don't know anything about the YB40?"

"Nope, I sure don't."

He didn't believe me, but that didn't matter. I was not going to tell him anything. I *couldn't* tell him anything. He knew I couldn't and I wouldn't and he didn't push the YB40 matter any further. Turned out that the interrogation overall was a piece of cake.

He let me go and I was escorted to a tiny cellblock about four feet wide and six feet long.

It was like the room they called the "cooler" in "The Great Escape," except even smaller.

It was August (1943) and the windows were nailed shut and the heat was turned on. It was hotter than hell. There was a button you could push and a flag would drop down. This was a signal to the guard that you wanted something. Most of the time, though, the guards just put the flag back up and ignored me.

One day, however, I pleaded with the guard, "I haven't had a bath in months." I guess he felt sorry for me and finally consented one day when his boss wasn't around. He let me out of my cell and escorted me to the shower. He stood there and watched me and kept yelling, "Hurry up, vite, vite." It felt so good that I could have stayed in there forever. But I didn't want to push my luck. Maybe this guy would do another favor for me someday, I thought.

The food I got in my cell was God-awful. It consisted of two pieces of stale bread with what looked like axle grease between them. And I never did figure out what that black stuff really was.

One day a German, wearing a Luftwaffe uniform and a Red Cross armband, came into my cell. He said he was from the Red Cross. He gave me a questionnaire with nothing but military questions on it. I told him I couldn't answer any of these questions. Then he became belligerent. "You must! If you don't I can't notify your family that you are alive and well," he exclaimed.

"Okay, Okay," I said. "I'll answer one military question – that's all. But you must promise me on your word as a German officer that you'll send word to my family."

He said, "I promise."

So after the question, "command" I wrote, "Bomber."

"That's not fair," he said.

"But you gave me your word!"

He shrugged his shoulders, looked away for a second, and then said, "All right. You win."

Then he asked me if I wanted some Schnapps.

"You mean beer," I said, excitedly. "Real beer?"

He handed me a bottle of beer and quickly left the cell. I sipped it; savored it. It was the best beer I'd ever had!

I spent three days there in the "cooler" before being moved to another transient camp that was up on a hill. I was put in a room with twelve other guys who were recent prisoners, too. There was only one bed and one table so we just all sat around on the floor. The other guys didn't trust me at first. Because I was in civilian clothes they thought I might be a ringer (a spy for the Germans). But it didn't take me long to convince them that I was just one of "them."

The Red Cross finally showed up at that camp and brought us boxes of food. We also received shoes, toothbrushes, and shaving stuff. This wasn't the Ritz, but it was sure nicer than my days in solitary confinement back at Fresnes - until I had to go to the bathroom. Right after the Red Cross left I banged on the door and yelled that I had to go to the John. Finally, a squirt guard (smaller than me) came to the door with a pistol in his hand. I told him I had to go to the John. He started hollering, right in my face. (These guys were always hollering.) I went nose to nose with him and started hollering right back: "I have to go to the John." That pissed him off bad. He took out his pistol and fired it into the floor, right at my feet. That made me even angrier, and he could see it. I was with twelve other Americans, and I was feeling frisky (I wasn't alone anymore). The squirt guard, sensing my anger, relented and let me go to the bathroom.

After a couple of days we were sent down the hill to the main camp, where there was a mess hall. I don't remember whether it was buffet style or if we were served. (Can't imagine that they would serve us, though). Anyhow, I remember having a great time. And the food wasn't half bad!

That evening they let us mingle with the British prisoners. They were the craziest guys I'd ever been around. And they loved to sing. Their lyrics were off the charts filthy; and their limericks were absolutely hilarious. We sang along with them and screamed with laughter.

We were in this camp about a week and I don't have a single recollection about where I slept. Since there was only one bed in our room, I guess I slept on the floor.

I do remember, though, that we were loaded on a train early one morning and told we were heading to our permanent camp in East Germany.

I was sick the whole trip. Because of my change in diet, a severe case of diarrhea escorted me all the way.

10

MY NEW "HOME:" STALAG LUFT III

My official papers for Stalag Luft III

We arrived at Stalag Luft III in late August 1943. They put me in a so-called "infirmary" with a couple of other guys who were also sick. The Red Cross had special parcels for sick prisoners that settled down my runaway bowels. In a couple of days I was "good to go" and entered the main camp.

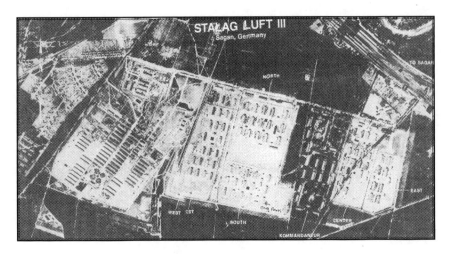

Bird's Eye view of Stalag Luft III

Stalag Luft III was near Sagan (now in Poland) about 100 miles southeast of Berlin. It was composed of five compounds: center, east, north, south and west. I was in the center compound and it was there that we started our "combines." Ten to twelve guys formed a group and shared Red Cross parcels. We cooked food communally. After about a month, we moved into the brand new south compound. The Germans segregated us from the British because they thought we got along too well. The British were housed in the north and east compounds. The Americans were in the center, south and west compounds. Eventually there were approximately 10,000 flying officers in Stalag Luft III: 6,000 Americans and 4,000 British. Each compound had about 2,000 prisoners. When we transferred from the center to the south, we walked, en masse. There were no formal orders. We just ran and grabbed a room. My group got Block 136, Room 6 at one end of the compound.

Typical room in Stalag Luft III; built for six kriegies, but ended up housing sixteen of us

We were right at the perimeter of the counting field, where they counted us every day. It was a big area, too; big enough to play softball on. Considering my previous experiences with the Gestapo in Paris, the prison wasn't all that bad. We really were never threatened. Our main problem was getting enough to eat.

We got one Red Cross parcel per week that equated to about 900 calories a day. It weighed about eight pounds and contained a can of corn beef, a can of salmon and a can of Spam. There was a small cylinder of liver pate and a can of powdered milk, which became known as KLIM-milk spelled backwards. KLIM became very valuable because of the can it came in. Seemed that we made everything out of KLIM cans. The parcel also contained crackers, five or six packs of cigarettes, a slender slip of lemon pills for Vitamin C, and a container of jelly.

Red Cross parcel with "KLIM" can at center top

In early September we were given two pieces of stationary, two envelopes and three V-mails. The V-mails were little self-mailers that folded twice into the size of a postcard. I wrote to Doris and my mother and told them of my fate. I told them about my disastrous flight on March 8, how I was harbored by the French, and then caught and arrested by the Gestapo in Paris. I assured them that I was not injured, and that I was being treated OK at Stalag Luft III. I knew, though, that it would take months before they received these letters, maybe not even until after Christmas. No telling what they'd heard from the War Department . . .

WESTERN UNION

NE 40 GOVT 2 EXTRA=NEW YORK NY SEP 11 1125A
MRS EMMABELLE K EDRIS=
127 KNICKERBOCKER RD DELIVER DON'T FONDNMZ=

CORRECTED REPORT RECEIVED THROUGH INTERNATIONAL RED CROSS STATES YOUR SON FIRST LIEUTENANT WARREN P EDRIS A PRISONER OF WAR OF THE GERMAN GOVERNMENT AND NOT KILLED IN ACTION AS REPORTED IN MY TELEGRAM OF TEN JULY LETTER FOLLOWS=

ULIO THE ADJUTANT GENERAL WASHINGTON DC

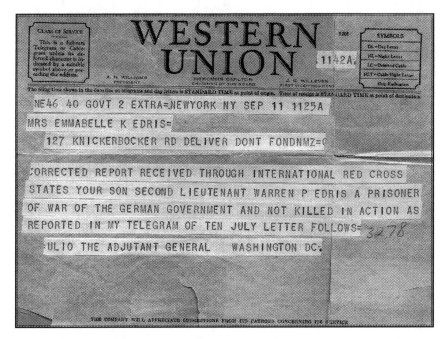

When the Western Union girl saw the good news she picked up the phone and called my mother. When Mom heard the news, she started screaming and fainted to the floor. My sister Helen heard the commotion, ran into the kitchen and grabbed the phone. The Western Union girl repeated the message to Helen: "First Lieutenant Edris IS NOT DEAD."

When Helen finally got Mother revived, she grabbed a bottle of booze and ran down the road hollering, "HE'S ALIVE! HE'S ALIVE."

The War Department contacted my mother the next day, Sept. 12, 1943, and gave her my address at Stalag Luft III

Efangenennummer 1969

Lager-Bezelchnung, Stalag Luft III, Germany

She and Doris sent out letters the same day. Unbeknownst to us, our letters were crossing in the mail.

There was nothing I could do now, but live one day at a time . . . and try to survive.

Getting enough to eat was a good way to start.

We took turns pulling KP duty and peeling German potatoes. And we "kreigies" -POWs in Germany were all called kreigies, which is short for the German word Kriegsgefangenen, which means prisoner of war. We could really peel potatoes, too. We made damn sure we got just the skin and nothing else. And we kept a roster of whose turn it was to eat the skins, where we thought most of the vitamins were.

Our breakfast consisted of bread and jam, but we avoided the Red Cross margarine, which was horrible. It was called, "Miami Margarine" and it stunk to high heavens. The German margarine was far superior. We actually used the American stuff for grease.

I decided we needed dessert on a regular basis and anointed myself as the dessert cook, or poor man's "pastry chef."

We had prunes, raisins, crackers, and sugar. Perfect ingredients for the pie I planned to make.

Our "kitchen" contained a communal pot that was about a foot high and eight inches in diameter. We also had a tiny square stove in one corner of the room-about a foot square four feet high that we used for heating and cooking. The goons supplied us with bricks made from powdered coal dust that was compressed into bricks. There just wasn't enough coal dust, though, to help heat our quarters. So . . . we used most of our coal bricks for cooking.

The pie project was a team effort. The KPs pitted the prunes and I dumped them into the pot, along with some water. Cracker crumbs were added to stiffen the mixture.

While the prune mixture bubbled away, one of my fellow kriegies, R. O. Henley, made an extra big pie tin. "Ro" was our "tin man" and made many containers from KLIM cans. The one he made for me was eighteen inches long, a foot wide and two inches deep; also made out of KLIM cans.

Drawing I did of my friend and fellow kriegie R. O. 'Ro' Henley

Other kriegies rolled out crackers with a coffee cup until they were a nice, almost powdery consistency. We mixed the margarine (German) and the crackers to make a crust. We also had a regular, communal stove in the center of the barracks that was augmented with KLIM cans that we used for special cooking. We also had a communal KLIM can oven whose firebox had KLIM cans attached to it (by a very clever kriegie), for which to blow hot air through the oven. That's where I cooked the crust.

I took powdered milk, sugar, and margarine and kneaded the ingredients together with a little water and then beat it until it became sort of a whipped cream. It was very heavy and not what you could call "fluffy." And it was very rich. The crust was now ready so I dumped the prune mixture into the pie tin. When it cooled I poured the whipped cream on top of it. That was our dessert and it was outstanding. We couldn't eat that much of it because it was so sweet. So we stashed the rest of it for later. It was my first test after becoming the "self-proclaimed" dessert cook. And I was quite proud of myself!

When new "purges" (kriegies) arrived at camp, we all went down to the gate to greet them, looking for friends. "What the hell are you doing here," we'd often say to guys we had flown with. Occasionally we'd get a few "newcomers" to our block. Our twelve-man room eventually housed sixteen men. It was designed to house eight.

The new guys believed anything we told them. They were numb, dazed and hungry. Some people say that stomachs don't shrink, but I'm not so sure. I do know that you can get somewhat used to being hungry. I know I did.

We also told the new guys that we didn't want to hear their "there I was," shot-down stories but once. We've all told those stories enough, so once will be enough. On the other hand, however, you can talk about your sex life all you want. One guy took us up on it and said he'd slept with a famous Hollywood movie star. Yeah, right, we all thought.

Kriegies a couple of doors down decided to pull a dirty trick on a new guy. They set it up so one kriegie was lying on the second sack with a sheet over his head. The new guy came in and sat down at the table. One of the guys in the room said, "Okay, go ahead and tell us your 'there I was' story." The new guy started talking about how he was shot down, in great detail. Every now and then some guys would lift the sheet and sprinkle the guy who was under it with powered milk from a saltshaker. They did this every few minutes. Finally, the new kriegie said, "What in the hell are you guys doing?"

With head hung low, one of the jokester kriegies said, "Well, poor Joe died last week. Like you, he was one of the new guys. We don't know what he died of; he just, well . . . died. So . . . we're sprinkling talcum powder on him to keep the smell down."

"So why don't you just get the Germans to bury him?" asked the new guy.

"No way," the jokester quipped. "We don't want to give up his Red Cross parcels!"

The head guard of the south compound for our barracks was a guy named Glimlitz, who was the equivalent of a master sergeant. A flier in World War I, Glimlitz was hard, but fair. He didn't bother you unless you did something wrong. And then off to the cooler you went.

He was always practicing his slang English, so he could understand us better. Guards occasionally crawled up under our barracks just to eavesdrop. That's why we set stiff rules on who were allowed to talk to them. We weren't allowed to use the word "escape," we used the letter "X" instead. We couldn't use the word "radio," either, although someone had sneaked one into our compound. All we could say to the guards was, "Good morning, good afternoon, and good evening." This way, no one could accidentally say something that could be taken the wrong way. Again, only designated kriegies were allowed to talk to the "goons."

"Goons" were what POWs called guards in German prison camps. Goons were often WW I veterans, or younger men who were more or less at the bottom of the German military food chain.

We practiced etiquette of sorts in the camp. We always knocked on the door before entering a person's room. Glimlitz always carried a prang, a long slender tool, that he poked around with. He would knock on the door with it, waltz in, and say, "Good afternoon, gentlemen."

We'd respond by saying, "Good afternoon," and that's all we'd say. Glimlitz would walk around the room, trying out his English slang on us, but we wouldn't say anything to him.

Some guys in another room told us a hilarious story about Glimlitz.

One day as he stood at the door to leave their room, he turned around, shook his finger and said, "You think I know fuck nothing. But I know fuck all!"

We almost fell on the floor laughing.

Comic relief helped salve our homesickness.

II

THE SO-CALLED CAMP HOSPITAL

There was a hospital of sorts in the German part of the camp. I came down with a severe toothache one day and informed one of the goons. He said he would inform the "hospital" and put me on a waiting list. Months later, I was standing in line waiting to see the dentist. While waiting, I looked out the window and saw what we called the "Honey Wagon." It was the vehicle that the sewage from our johns was pumped into. To my horror, they were spraying this human excrement onto the cabbages as fertilizer. Anyhow, I finally got to the door of the dentist's office and looked inside. They were holding down a guy who was screaming at the top of his lungs. The dentist was pulling one or more of his teeth with no novacane, or any kind of numbing whatsoever. In contrast, a prisoner with a piece of shrapnel in his brain was taken to a nearby hospital where he was operated on by one of the best brain surgeons in Europe, a French doctor who also had been captured by the Germans.

Generally speaking, though, it was just not a good idea to get sick. Except for my first three days at Stalag Luft III, when I had severe diarrhea, I was never sick a day, not even with a cold. In the winter it was always cold and damp and we could never get warm. We went to bed every night wearing every stitch of clothes we had, just to stay halfway warm. We each had two blankets and checkered sheets that weren't washed but about every other month. We didn't have pillows.

"Ro" Henley, who was in the sack across from me, came up with a clever idea. He shredded newspapers and sewed them between his two blankets for insulation. For thread, he used unraveled wool socks. For his needle, he used a sliver of wood, and punched a little hole in the top, and sewed the blankets together. It worked beautifully.

We did everything we could to stay warm. It's a wonder none of us came down with pneumonia!

Being that sick, though, would have kept us out of Stalag Luft III to start with. Severely sick or wounded prisoners were never assigned to that camp.

In early '44 a letter from my mother, dated September 12, 1943, left me dumbfounded. "When we got the good news, Junior, we took the Gold Star out of the window." "What the hell is this all about," I asked Ro. He looked at the letter and said, "Don't you know what this means you nut? A Gold Star means you were dead!"

Then it dawned on me that I was listed as killed in action. God, how many months had my family and Doris had to live with this? How horrible for them to think that I'm dead and then be told that I was alive. What a rollercoaster ride.

They believed I was dead. Now they know I'm alive.

Dying is for another day.

That's what I told Doris and my family, too. Although I was never dead to start with, I felt like I had been given a second chance at life. And I was going to do every thing possible to survive this hell-on-earth place called Stalag Luft III. "I'm living for the day I can hold you in my arms," I told Doris in the first letter she received from me after she got the good news that I was still alive. Our letters were few and far between, however. It was taking forever to get mail, sometimes three or four months. I cherished my letters from Doris, and read them over and over.

"I thought I would pass out when your mother called to say you were alive. I screamed and jumped up and down . . . and called everybody I knew," Doris wrote in her letter dated Sept. 12, 1943. (Received in early January, 1944.)

We didn't get mail regularly, nor did we always get our personal parcels. The government sent my mother, as next of kin, little slips to put on the boxes she shipped to me. She could pack up to ten pounds in these boxes. She got another kind of slip she could use to mail to the cigarette companies. American Tobacco Company would then send four cartons of Chesterfields (that my mother paid fifty cents a carton for) directly to me in the prison camp. One enterprising kriegie figured out a nifty use for the cigarette packaging: protecting our precious photographs. He would take the cellophane wrappers off the packs and soak them in hot water. Somehow the hot water allowed him to peel off the stiff outer layer, leaving just a thin piece of cellophane. Then using a mixture of flower and water for glue, we wrapped the cellophane around our photos and glued it to the back. I couldn't wait for my next batch of pictures to arrive!

Another tobacco company, R. J. Reynolds in Winston-Salem, N.C. also provided more than just smokes to us. But they did it on purpose. They meticulously cut cigarettes, Camels, and inserted tiny compasses by hand. We were notified by our little home made secret radios that these cigarettes were on their way. They never got to us however, because the Germans found out about them. And that was it. No more Camel cigarettes were allowed in the camps.

Doris, who was working in Raleigh, N. C. at the time, went to great lengths to put together parcels that would be most valuable and useful. She and her co-workers put a lot of effort into these ten -pound parcels. She would ask me in letters about them, but I had no idea what she was talking about. These parcels obviously were intercepted by the Germans, and put to good use . . . by them.

We had a store in the camp called "Foodacco." If you had extra stuff you could store it there and use it for bartering. A ledger was kept there, and everything was priced by points. A can of KLIM, in other words, might be worth 500 points. You could accumulate and buy with your points, or swap things.

Carl Alexander, who was a navigator, was one of my roommates. He had worked for a grocery chain and knew everything about food. One of the first things he did after he arrived was write his mother and request a bottle of vanilla tablets. None of us had ever heard of such a thing. It took six months, but they finally came. He then became the richest guy in camp because we traded all kind of stuff for these delicious seasonings.

When personal parcels arrived the guard opened them right in front of you. While he was examining the contents, he would start eating your candy, or whatever.

There wasn't always candy, though. Mothers liked to send healthy stuff, too. One day a guy's parcel contained nothing but six cans of tomato juice. He was so mad.

"Why did she waste all that space for tomato juice?" he whined. So he kept one can and took the other five to Foodacco. He got maybe fifty points for the whole lot. Back in his room he discovered his can didn't contain tomato juice at all. It was beer! She had peeled off tomato juice labels and stuck them on beer cans. He ran back to Foodacco to retrieve the other five cans, but they were already gone!

12

LET US ENTERTAIN YOU

We had a little wind-up phonograph that made its rounds to every room in the south compound. All of us enjoyed it. When the lights went out at night we'd play Benny Goodman. Records came to us from the Salvation Army and other charitable organizations. One record had a Bing Crosby label on it, but it was actually a Spike Jones recording: "Heil! Heil! Right in the Fuerher's Face!" We loved it. We would play that record over and over and scream laughing!

We loved to play cards but no one had sent us any. So we made our own out of cardboard. But it didn't take long for us to figure out which card was which, with the bent corners, stains, creases, and the like.

We finally did get a real deck of cards, though, and that's when I learned how to play bridge. I was taught by one of my roommates, George Stier, who was a tournament bridge player in college. He was an expert no doubt, and I became one, too. I became his partner and we once made it to the quarter- finals in our camp tournament. We had fun and it was a great way to pass the time away. We didn't just sit around and play bridge, however, we ran a lot. Racing had become a fad around camp. One lap around the camp was one kilometer. We would bet an entire Red Cross parcel on these races, one room against the other.

There were other kinds of contests, too. One kriegie would say, "I can eat a whole Red Cross parcel in one twenty-four hour period." His roommates would go from room to room and take bets on whether or not he could do it.

One guy who said he could do it was Larry Connors, another bridge player, and a little guy.

So what he had to consume was a gallon of milk, a can of salmon, a can of corn beef, a can of spam, prunes, margarine, etc. in twenty-four hours. I remember everybody crowding around him. I remember his belly was so swollen that he looked pregnant. After his last swallow, he showed off by swishing water around in a bowl and drinking it. Part of the bet, of course, was that he had to keep the food down. And he did. He won a couple of Red Cross parcels for that feat.

It was harmless fun and the guards knew it. So they pretty much left us alone, which they did most of the time. If somebody got out of hand, though, and tried to escape, they would punish us all by rationing us to half parcels.

One day Glimlitz, our chief guard, (the guy who knows "fuck everything") was slowly pacing around the compound, hands behind his back. Just for fun, a couple of kriegies got behind him in lock step. Before long, there were ten more. And they kept coming, until there were more than 100 kriegies behind Glemlitz, all in lock step. He said, "Don't touch me," and then all the kriegies started to hum, "Russian Winter, Russian Winter," to the tune of "Volga Boatman." They were marching round and round. A guy even pulled out his trumpet and started playing. It was hilarious. Finally, Glimlitz came to a dead stop and a couple kriegies piled right into him. He grabbed them by the collar and marched them off to the cooler.

It's amazing how much diverse talent we had among our 2,000 guys in the south compound. So much talent in fact, that we had our own band. Or actually, you could call it an orchestra. It was a twelve-piece outfit that called themselves the "Luftbansters (the German press called us the Luftgansters). The leader was a musician from the renowned Paul Whiteman orchestra, one of the original big bands in the "Roaring Twenties."

And we had an arranger from NBC, who made music manuscripts and transcribed instruments' parts from recordings to paper. He wrote the music for each instrument.

We built a theater from the crates that held Red Cross parcels. Some of the charities provided the instruments; and we also bought stuff from pay through the POW Geneva convention rules.

On opening night the Luftbansters were unbelievably good. They were as good as any band back in the States. It was the only band in Stalag Luft III and the Germans allowed it to play for the British in the north compound. One day, as they were leaving for the south compound, the Luftbansters stopped and played "God Save the King." It was a sight to behold. The British came from everywhere and stood there at attention. The Germans weren't happy, though, and temporarily confiscated all the instruments. They returned them later, however, and our band was allowed to visit and play at all the compounds.

We even had a professional makeup artist in our barracks name Geiger. He was the guy who did all the makeup for our plays. We had a fair skinned, blond headed guy in our barracks that Geiger thought he could make up to look like a beautiful woman. It took a while, but we finally convinced this guy to become our lead "female" singer in the band. Geiger even showed him how to walk and throw his hips around.

When he/she showed up on the stage fully made up and sporting the blue gown we almost tore the theatre down. We screamed and yelled and went nuts. He only knew one song and sang it in a throaty, torch-singer voice. We cried out for more. We wouldn't let him leave the stage. We made him sing the same song over and over. He did things like grab the curtain and pull it up and down between his legs. We all went berserk!

Then we came up with another use for him/her.

There was a guy in the room next to us who slept all the time. We used to have lotteries where we threw in a cigarette or something, betting on how long this guy would stay in the sack. Roommates secretly logged him in and out. The guy who guessed the correct number of hours would win the pot.

One day we had the man/woman in the blue gown crawl in bed with "Mr. Sleepy Head." When he woke up and turned over he was in for the surprise of his life. He started yelling and screaming. We thought he was going to have a heart attack!

13

TAKE ME OUT TO THE BALLGAME

Each barracks had a softball team. We had an American League and a National League and it was pretty entertaining to watch. Some of these guys were really good. Sometimes the ball would go past the warning rail and someone would have to get permission from a guard to retrieve it and throw it back into play.

When we were in center compound and mixed with the British we were introduced to Rugby. This was a new game to most of us so we wanted to learn how to play it.

They tried to teach us the game, but we screwed it up pretty good. Instead of lateraling the Rugby ball like you're supposed to, our guys put their heads down, stiff armed and tried to run with it. When they got in a jam they just stopped and kicked it. The Germans put an end to our Rugby careers. Too many of our guys ended up in the "infirmary."

14

A WALK IN THE WOODS

The barracks at Stalag Luft III had been cleared from a thick forest of giant pine trees, leaving nothing but bare ground and tree stumps. One of our jobs was to get rid of these stumps. The goons brought us a stump puller that had two long levers and two claws to wrap around the roots at the base of the stump. We'd get about three guys on each of these levers, pulling straight down to pry the stump out of the ground. With the stumps, we knew we had fuel for winter.

The stump puller was what they loaned us on our "parole." Parole meant we would not violate the purpose of the parole for escape purposes.

So in some cases, parole meant up to ten of us could take a walk in the woods with guards. It was quite a treat to feel some "controlled" freedom. It was good for our morale.

15

THOUGHTS OF ESCAPE

Flood lights swept across the camp all night long. And if the guards saw you trying to crawl under the wires, they would mow you down. There were also German Shepherds roaming the camp at night.

As a deterrent to escaping, the guards called a bunch of us together one day in the presence of a guard dog. A guard, all padded up, came sneaking around the corner. Then . . . the dog leader, "hunt fuehrer," barked a command at the dog. It worked. The dog jumped on the guard and went right at his throat. When he'd knocked the escape guard down, the dog stood over him and growled. They told us if we ever got caught in this situation, not to move.

We really had the run of the camp as long as we adhered to the rules. There was a double fence of barbed wire around the compound, ten feet high with rolled wire in between. There was a warning rail ten feet before the fence. If anyone went over this warning rail they could be shot. They didn't want us anywhere near the fence. Otherwise, though, we had free reign within the camp.

When a new prisoner came in he was interviewed by an American officer, who explained the rules of the camp. He said if you ever see or hear anything unusual to just keep walking; don't stop and stare, just keep walking. I heard Morse code being tapped out one day when I was walking, and I never slowed down.

Unless there was a really good opportunity for a sudden escape, we were to stay put. For a planned escape, like digging tunnels, we were supposed to get permission. Otherwise, we might interfere with another escape plan by stumbling into someone else's tunnel project, thus tipping off the goons.

There was an organization in camp called the "X Committee." "X" meant the word escape, which we were not allowed to say.

Besides digging tunnels, another way to escape was called a "wire job." One of the several kriegies who tried it, with permission, was a guy named John Lewis from Goldsboro, N.C. He lived in our barracks, which was as close as you could get to the wire-maybe just thirty feet to the warning rail and another ten feet to the wire. For a wire job, you used homemade wire cutters. You took four stakes about two feet high that were notched on the top. You'd crawl to the first barbed wire and clip it. Then you had the coiled wire to get through before you could get to the outside wire. You'd take the first two stakes, prop up the coil and put the stakes in the ground. You'd crawl a foot or so and put up the other two stakes and you'd have a tunnel beneath the coil of barbed wire. Then you'd clip the outer wire and off you'd go.

John Lewis got to the outer wires. He was on his belly, clipping the last wires when a strolling guard came along. John said later that it scared the guard as much as it scared him. The guard jumped, and John immediately threw the wire cutters back into the camp. Knowing very little German, John looked up at the guard and yelled, "Nix shysen," (which is phonetic for, "Don't shit"). "Don't shoot" in German is "Nix Sheesan!"

The guard threw down his rifle and started laughing hysterically.

John didn't escape, but he lived.

The morning roll call, called "appel," was usually at seven or eight in the morning. Each block lined up four deep, and the officer went along the line, counting us. An enlisted man walked behind, double-checking to ensure there were no blank spaces. The American senior officer also was there with his adjutant. When the count was complete, the German officer would salute and leave the camp area.

The main stumbling block for a successful escape was being able to cover for the guys for a couple of days to give them a head start. To accomplish this, we would carry parts of mannequins under our clothes as we marched to the field. As we milled about, we would assemble the mannequins in the middle of the group. Kriegies on either side of the escaped guys space held the mannequin up. They'd have a head, a hat, a jacket and a pair of pants. They covered for a guy named "Shorty" Spire that way for several days before the goons caught on. He almost made it.

We got into trouble when we did things like this, of course. Our rations got cut in half and they would restrict our activities, mostly by taking away our athletic equipment.

The movie "The Great Escape," occurred in the British north compound, just on the other side of us. A single wire separated the compounds.

Although the Americans helped build the famous tunnels called Tom, Dick and Harry, only the British ended up escaping. That's because the Americans had been moved to the south compound.

All told, seventy-six British officers got out. After being captured by the Gestapo, fifty of the officers were shot. Upon hearing this news, Colonel Goodrich ordered us to have a "disorderly appel." When they came to count us nobody would line up. After one look, the German commandant ordered all of his guards out of camp. They returned one hour later armed with submachine guns. That made Colonel Goodrich change his mind pretty quickly . . . and he called for an "orderly appel!" I guess he thought they'd really shoot us.

16

SIRENS! SIRENS!

One day in the spring of 1944 the sirens went off which was very unusual. Rare were daylight raids in East Germany. A whole wing of B-17s flew over and it was quite a sight! Bright, uncamouflaged . . . shining in the sun. They were targeting a FW-190 plant a few miles from Sagan.

One of our guys was watching from the doorway when a guard outside the fence shot him in the mouth, killing him instantly. In a hearing later, we learned that the guard then planted the spent shell outside the fence, to make the shooting appear justified. Usually the guards got just a slap on the wrist for this kind of behavior, and transferred to another base. We think that's what happened in this case, too. No big deal for the Germans.

Alarms were not unusual during my stay at Stalag Luft III, especially at night. The British were conducting these raids. Of course the Germans turned off the lights during these raids. One night a goon got pissed off during a raid and fired a few shots into our barracks just to scare us. It worked.

It was worse in the next room to ours, though. Colonel Stevenson, playing cards in there by the light of homemade candles, was hit in both legs. The same bullet actually went through one leg and then through the other leg. It actually ripped about three inches of bone from one of his thighs. He was screaming and hollering and yelling, "God. I've been hit. I've been hit!"

We gathered in the hallway in the dark, stumbled in, and pulled him out of his room. We took him to one of the middle rooms where it was safe. We put two tables together and hoisted him up onto them. He was a big guy and his legs were soaked with blood. We started cutting off his pant leg. He coolly said, "Before I pass out please know I got hit in BOTH legs."

It was a bloody, gory mess. We hollered out the window, "Guard, guard!" Finally they brought an officer, escorted by a German Shepherd. We were lined up on either side of the wall and the goon "walked the gauntlet" We were furious, but there was nothing we could do. The goons seemed nervous and trigger-happy so it was best that we just stayed cool. They finally came and took Colonel Stevenson away. Months later he returned with a very severe limp. They had patched him up but hadn't added an extension where the bone was destroyed.

Word got to Colonel Stevenson that I could do Jewish dialect. We had the poem Hiawatha, "By the shores of Gitchee Gumee . . ." in Jewish dialogue.

One night the Colonel ordered me to come to his room and recite the poem. He went into sheer hysterics. I was his friend for life!

These lighter moments kept everything in perspective for me. It was important to try and stay positive. So I was glad I could cheer up Colonel Stevenson. I mean this guy's been crippled for life by a random shooting from a lunatic goon, and he's able to laugh. He was an inspiration to me . . . being able to take his wounds in stride, and knowing that he could have taken that bullet to his heart.

I was thankful that night that that bullet hadn't hit me. Maybe it was a sign that I was going to get out of this mess alive after all.

Prisoners of war take it one day at a time. Unlike regular prisoners, POWs don't get their sentences shortened by good behavior. Our behavior, though, could be suspect at times. Risky would actually be a better word. Or stupid.

In the summer of 1944 some fellow kriegies and I developed a "deadly' craving for French fries!

17

THE GREAT POTATO HEIST

There was a "cookhouse" in our compound where they heated water for us in the morning. The cookhouse also had a cellar where potatoes were stored by the truckload.

Early one morning a truck backed up to the cellar and the driver pushed a coal shute into its window. The window was below ground level and contained a circular well about two feet below the window itself. As the driver shoveled potatoes into the chute I noticed some of them were falling into the well. When he was finished shoveling he filled the well with straw to keep cold out of the cellar.

What I saw was a gold mine of potatoes and my mouth started watering. Problem was, though, that the heist could only be done at night when we were confined to our blocks.

Plus, our doors were bolted which meant we'd have to crawl through the window. Another problem: The window faced directly across from the guard tower where the goon was perched with his machine gun and searchlight. Armed with Red Cross boxes and daredevil mentalities three of us kriegies took turns dodging the searchlight and zigzagging to our prey, which was at the far end of the compound. Miraculously, none of us was shot, nor attacked by the strolling German Shepherds. We had the grease and we had our little stove. And now we had our potatoes, ready to peel and deep fry into French fries that we had literally risked out lives for.

18

1944 WINDS DOWN

The rest of the summer was less eventful. I don't recall concocting another scheme as dangerous as the French fry caper.

I daydreamed of summers long past; of splashing around in the Atlantic with my Mom and Dad and my sisters Helen and Lucille. I longed for the day Doris and I could get married and raise a family. I prayed to survive this mess and live a long and normal life.

As summer transitioned into fall (and it was hard to tell the difference in the gloomy, gray landscape of Sagan) we did all we could to avoid total boredom. Bridge games, checkers, chess and poker games helped. Then there were the big events such as "big band" concerts and stage plays.

Packages from home were becoming larger and more plentiful, signaling the onset of the holiday season. They contained more photos than usual, mingled in with luxuries like cigarettes and chocolates.

One way or the other I believed this would be my last Christmas in Stalag Luft III.

19

THE FORCED MARCH

JANUARY 13, 1945

The long-awaited Russian offensive in the east and northeast started today. There has been a great deal of speculation as to how far they will have to go to finish up the War and how long it will take them.

JANUARY 25, 1945

A tremendous amount of excitement is all over the camp. Artillery fire was heard from the east.

During the past twelve days the Russians have been moving at a steady clip. As of today they are approximately fifty miles from Sagan. Optimism is very high.

JANUARY 27, 1945

A stage play, "You Can't Take It With You," was being presented tonight. I didn't go because I wanted a quiet evening alone to read. I had been reading only an hour or so when my roommates came bursting in the door. They told me Colonel Goodrich stopped the play and told everyone to return to their barracks and be ready to evacuate in half an hour. Boy, what a bombshell! We had been preparing for this by making makeshift knapsacks and kit bags, but the majority of us never thought the goons would evacuate us. There were too many plausible reasons against it. We kriegies were not at all fit for a forced march. Hell, we weren't fit to march ten kilometers. Plus, they didn't have enough men to guard us. There would just be too many chances to escape. This (march) was a surprise to us all.

It was chaos. Everyone was rushing around and trying to get the most valuable stuff assembled, especially warm clothing. And we had been issued seven Red Cross parcels that day. What a shame we didn't have time to bash them. We split up what bread we had cut and made some thick spread for once. I had two pieces of bread, one with an inch of honey on top and the other with a whole can of strawberry jam-a kriegie's dream. We had no time to make anything hot.

We were assembled outside about an hour later - around 9:15 p.m. - by blocks, with all our equipment on our backs. I brought two "saddlebags" (homemade out of a G.I. shirt), three changes of underwear, two handkerchiefs, five pairs of socks, two Army ration "D" bars (chocolate), one loaf of goon bread, two boxes of cheese, one bag of sugar, one bag of prunes and one can of corn beef. Also, a small sewing kit, my toilet articles, one towel, my two logbooks, practically all of Doris' pictures, about a hundred of her letters, and two cartons of cigarettes. Oh yes, I also packed a container of sulfathiazole to use on my infected big toe. A case of gangrene was the last thing I needed.

The worst thing of all was what we had to leave behind. We had quite a store of food for once because we had gone back on full parcels. If we'd had anytime to prepare anything we really could have had a tremendous stash of food. Too bad, since we all had lost quite a bit of weight due to weeks of half parcels. We also left a large Red Cross carton full of cigarettes, which had accumulated over a period of a year.

We did manage to burn quite a few so the goons wouldn't end up with them. I had thrown away what I had on and was dressed in "dress" greens: shirt, trousers and battle jacket. Those were the only outer garments I had for the march, besides my G.I. overcoat and scull cap.

We started marching about 10:00 p.m., destination unknown. We had no idea how far we had to walk, or how long it was going to take. We did know one thing, however: The Russians were coming, and from all appearances, fast.

Luckily the weather that night was fair and not too cold. But that changed. The temperature dropped rapidly as the night wore on . . . and snow began to fall.

What a sight it was to see a bunch of us kriegies marching along, backs bent slightly forward from the weight of our packs. Judging by the size of our packs, I got the impression we were leaving Sagan for good. There were 10,000 POWs on this march, 6,000 American flying officers and 4,000 RAF officers. As we passed the outer border some of the censors, who were women, were standing at the gate, crying. It was the closest I had been to a woman in over a year.

We marched in blocks and tried to keep fairly close together. My friend Don Roehn and myself stuck very close, sharing food and keeping each other company the whole way.

We were all in pretty high spirits when we started out but were sinking fast. The night had turned so bitter cold that my gloves had become useless. My hands felt like they were freezing off. And my feet were sopping wet, too! The snow had started coming down pretty good, probably half a foot already.

About four in the morning on January 28, 1945, we stopped in an open field (one thing I'll never forgive the goons for) where the wind was literally howling. Cold wasn't the word for it.

We were stopped so the goons could give us a ration of food: A hunk of bread. We were made to stand there about an hour. By the time we started walking again, my hands and feet were throbbing and sharp pains were rushing through my shoulder blades.

It was about this time that I started seeing discarded clothing, log books, cartons of cigarettes, blankets, etc. by the side of the road. The loads were getting heavy and guys were dumping stuff. We were in no condition for this march to start with.

After marching all night we reached Grassalton, thirty-one kilometers west of Sagan. We were quartered in barns and "rested" for about five hours. There must have been at least 500 kriegies in the barn Don and I were in. You couldn't walk a foot without stepping on somebody's face. I got no sleep there, but I did manage to change out of those soaking wet socks; and apply a glob of sulfathiazole to my infected toe.

The German woman who owned the barns happened by as Don and I were outside smoking a cigarette. And we sweet-talked her into doing a little "horse trading."

She boiled water for our Nescafe and we gave her a can in return. She was tickled pink.

We also gave her some chocolate and her eyes got as big as saucers.

Average German people didn't have anything when it came to decent food and clothing.

Don and I thanked her and headed back toward the barn where, outside, some of the kriegies were showing off their sleds. The goons allowed them to concoct these sleds from old ladders and boxes.

And they were perfect for carrying our baggage. Without these homemade sleds many of us wouldn't have finished the march.

We started out from Grasselton at 5:00 p.m., January 28, 1945 in a heavy snowstorm. A rumor was going around that the Russians were only a few kilometers down the road and had already captured Sagan. I knew it was probably false, but it helped my morale considerably.

Our sled had twelve men's baggage on it. Two of us would pull and two would push for periods of fifteen minutes. It was quite different from having to carry the things on our backs.

It was about this time that we started seeing quite a few German refugees in all sorts of horse-drawn conveyances, piled high with personal belongings. They were a sorry looking bunch, but I'm sure we were, too.

Things were getting worse. It was getting colder and colder and the only way I could keep slightly warm was by pushing or pulling the sled. Finally, the worst started happening. Men started to drop out. What an awful sight. There they would be, flat on their faces in the snow on the side of the road; their buddies by their sides, trying anything they could to help. The goons would not stop and we had to leave them behind for the wagon at the rear to pick up. I also was seeing more and more junk being thrown away.

One thing for sure: We no longer needed guards. It was all we could do to stay on our feet. I sure was thankful for the sugar lumps I brought with me. They gave some energy . . . and warmth.

I had hardly anything else to eat, though. Except for the goon bread, which was so dry and frozen that it made my mouth raw.

We marched twenty-seven kilometers and reached Muskau around 1:15 a.m. on January 29, 1945. I'll never forget the last hours of this trip. It was a nightmare.

In Muskau we were to be quartered in different sections of a factory, but when we arrived at our section we couldn't get in. It was that full. This was my first taste of men acting like animals. And when I looked around, another group was pushing and shoving toward a big fire that was burning in a furnace. Everybody was cold . . . and desperate.

About 200 of us had no place to go until a German officer came by and said he would lead us to another factory. The walk to the other factory took about fifteen minutes. And it was fifteen minutes of torture. My left hand was so cold it felt like it was burning.

We finally arrived and Don and I were the first to enter. It was a glass factory but almost bare of machines. Don and I were given a little corner with about enough room for one man. We laid out our blankets and dropped down on the cement floor, completely exhausted.

My hands seemed to be getting worse. Seriously frostbitten, no doubt. I learned from a book years ago that in this situation, body heat was the best thing for frostbite. And the only body heat I had was between my legs, and that's where I stuck my left hand. It worked. After about thirty minutes I had feeling in my hand again.

About that time my buddies Ro and Stick showed up and we made room for them in our little corner. Talk about body heat! We all four passed out and slept like babies.

We had marched fifty-eight kilometers from 10:00 p.m., January 27 to 1:15 a.m. January 29, 1945 with five hours rest and hardly any food. It wasn't until the next morning that the horror stories came drifting in. Out of the 2,000 men from the South Compound of Stalag Luft III, approximately fifteen to twenty passed out en route, eight went unconscious at the factory, and at least one went hysterical. There were dozens of cases of vomiting and hundreds of cases of blistered feet.

My hand seemed to be getting better and, ironically, my infected big toe was completely cured. Overall, I seemed relatively healthy.

The goon guards actually made out worse than many of us did. One died of a stroke and quite a few were severely frostbitten.

Believe it or not, the march wasn't without its humorous side. Our G.I.s, who marched to the rear of us, had to continually pick up a rifle of a guard who kept throwing it away. Finally one of the G.I.s carried the gun himself. And another G.I. carried the guard's pack for him.

On the morning after our night in the glass factory, Colonel Goodrich told us we were to stay put one more night, and then walk thirty-five more kilometers to Spremberg.

20

THE TRAIN RIDE FROM HELL

On Feb. 1, 1945, we stumbled into Spremburg and were herded into boxcars that were recently used for livestock. They were called "forty and eights" which meant they could hold forty men or eight horses. But there were more than forty men in my boxcar.

Probably more like sixty. We were stuck in there like sardines in a can. We couldn't even sit completely down or stand completely up. We could barely breathe, but unfortunately, our sense of smell was intact. And it was the most God-awful smell in the world. Imagine the combination: feces, vomit and urine odors so thick you could cut them with a knife. And there was hardly any ventilation in the boxcar, just two tiny windows near the ceiling, on opposite ends of the car. It was a three-day trip through a frozen, tundra-like landscape of scorched earth and bombed-out cities. There seemed to be no color at all. It was like we were extras in a black & white "B" movie being filmed in hell.

We rarely could even quench our thirst, much less go to the bathroom. The Germans let us out just once a day and what a sight it was: thousands of us defecating, throwing up and urinating in the snow while trembling, uncontrollably.

We got just enough food to keep us alive. A little dried piece of bread and a can of German pressed meat that had the texture of Spam. I had no idea what kind of meat it was. It could have been rat meat for all I knew (or cared). Add to that my last chocolate D-bar and a piece of American cheese and that's all I had for the whole trip. But it didn't matter. I was too scared and stressed out to be hungry.

Word had gotten out that Colonel Goodrich had authorized escape attempts and some thirty-two desperate souls took him up on it. But they were all captured within thirty hours.

I thought about an escape attempt but decided not to try. At least there was body heat in the boxcar. So I opted to stay put and not risk freezing to death, or getting shot!

I had lost track of time but I think it was around February 4th when we arrived in Moosburg, Germany. Moosburg was just north of Munich and just south of Nuremburg. The Germans were being squeezed from the east and west and the only place they could go was south. Hitler wanted to hold the British and American flying officers as hostages for bargaining power.

When we got to Moosburg the bastards wouldn't let us out of the boxcar. They kept us locked up in there all night. They finally let us out in the morning and marched us to a garish place called Stalag VIIA.

21

STALAG VIIA: HELL ON EARTH

Stalag VIIA was a hellhole if there ever was one. It was a rat nest of tiny compounds separated by barbed wire fences that separated old, rundown barracks. Although it had been designed to hold 14,000 French prisoners, it was now crammed with 130,000 POWs of all nationalities. Some barracks were no more than empty shells with dirt floors. Others consisted of two wooden buildings connected to a washroom with a few cold-water faucets. Wooden bunks were joined together into blocks of twelve, a method of cramming 500 men into a building originally intended to house 200, uncomfortably. All the buildings were hopelessly infected with vermin.

Bird's eye view of Stalag VIIA

The fleas were incredible. When I went to bed I stripped down naked and started from scratch. First, I'd turn my socks and pants inside out, then my underwear. As I went, I tore the fleas apart to kill them. As I 'de-fleaed' each piece of clothing, I'd hang it up high on a nail because the fleas couldn't jump that high.

We became experts on fleas; how high they can jump when they're loaded (with blood) and how high they can jump when they're empty.

After the nightly flea ritual, when all of our clothing was free of fleas, we'd put our clothes back on. Then, we'd stuff our pants inside our socks so the fleas couldn't crawl up our pant legs. Somebody would tie something around our sleeves and then we'd tie another piece of material around our necks.

I never had lice. Some of the guys did, but I didn't. I don't know why.

At first there were no Red Cross parcels. We had the 'green death' soup instead. I'm not sure what the green soup was made of, or even if it was supposed to be green. I was jealous of the guys who could eat it however, because they were at least getting something in their stomachs. All I remember eating at Moosburg until the Red Cross parcels arrived was bread. I was so hungry on a couple of occasions that I even ate grass. If goats and cows can eat grass, I thought, so can I. Let's just say it wasn't a good idea.

Some enterprising prisoner invented a "Kriegie burner." And then we all copied it. You took a little can and put it on a board. Then you built a little tunnel up to a wheel made out of tin . . . sort of like a propeller with a handle on it. When you turned the handle, it pumped air down into the little can underneath, sort of like a forge. It worked like a charm. We could burn green wood with it; or anything else for that matter.

Each compound was divided by the aforementioned barbed wire. The compound next to ours was full of Russian slave laborers. There was no Geneva Convention to protect the Russians. The Germans treated them worse than animals. We'd heard that the Russians weren't getting any fat at all in their diets, so George Stier and I decided to help. We cut a hole in the fence and sneaked into their compound. The smell in there was more horrible than I can describe.

We tried to communicate with a couple of Russians who were sitting on the floor when we noticed they had potatoes. That's when we pointed to the margarine we'd brought along. The Russians broke out in big smiles. They opened both ends of the can of margarine and pushed the stuff through in a big cylinder. They split it in half and each ate half. They made up for the fat they had been lacking in a hurry!

Rumor had it that the guards were scared to death of the Russians and wouldn't go near their barracks. If there was any trouble the Russians had to handle it themselves. But for some reason one day a guard entered the Russian barracks accompanied by his German Shepherd. The guard got out OK but the dog didn't fare as well. They threw its bones out later. We all assumed they ate the dog.

I'll never forget one of the Russian slave laborers. He went out with his work platoon every morning but there was something horribly different about him: He had no legs below his knees. He had tape wrapped around both stumps. He walked on those stumps along with the other Russians – like a midget.

It was a depressing sight. But everything about Stalag VIIA was depressing. How much longer could any of us survive in this unspeakable squalor? How much longer, God? How much longer?

The 14th Armored Division landed at Marseilles, France, on October 29, 1944. Within two weeks some of its elements were in combat, maintaining defensive positions along the Franco-Italian frontier. The Division moved north to Rambervillers on November 20 to take part in the VI Corps drive through the Vosges Mountains. Hard fighting at Gertwiller, Benfeld, and Barr cracked Nazi defenses, and the Division was on the Alsatian Plain by early December. Attacking across the Lauter River on December 12, it took Haguenau, moved across the Moder River and entered the Haguenau woods. On Christmas day the 14th was assigned defensive positions running south of Bitche near Neunhoffen. It thwarted the heavy German attack in the Bitche salient launched on New Year's Eve. Although forced to withdraw, the Division remained intact. With the failure of the Bitche attack, the enemy attempted to break through to Strasbourg by attacks at Hatten and Rittershoffen, but again the drive was halted by the 14th Armored in a furious defensive engagement in January 1945. After rest, rehabilitation, and defensive missions during February and early March, the Division returned to the offensive on March 15. Then it drove across the Moder River, cracked through the Siegfried Line, and by the end of the month had captured Germersheim on the Rhine. On Easter Sunday, April 1, 1945, the 14th moved across the Rhine near Worms and continued pursuit of the retreating enemy through Lohr, Germunden, Neustadt, and Hammelburg. In its final thrust, the Division raced to the Danube, crossed at Ingolstadt, and pushed on across the Isar river to Moosburg.

22

LIBERATION DAY

On the morning of April 29, 1945, elements of the 14th Armored Division of General George Patton's 3rd Army began attacking the SS troops guarding Stalag VIIA.

We could hear the bullets. One of our guys stood up to see what was going on and was knocked off his stool by a bullet that luckily ricocheted off the barred window. He wasn't hurt at all. The 30-caliber bullet actually ended up stuck in his shirt. On a knoll off in the distance we could see three American tanks approaching, guns rotating, looking for targets. Over to the left, about a half-mile away, was a church tower with a steeple in the heart of Moosburg. And in the steeple stood a diehard German with a bazooka that I think they called "The Iron Fist." We could see the flames of fire coming out of the belfry window. He was firing away at Patton's tanks. I thought to myself, "What a moron." Then we saw the guns on the tanks rotate toward the church. One shot blew the tower to bits, German and all. Later that day it was all over. A Sherman tank came bursting through the main entrance, knocking down the barbed wire and plowing through the gate. A bunch of us jumped on the tank. It was sheer pandemonium. The G.I.s in the tank finally figured out what we wanted: souvenirs. They obliged me when I asked for some 30-caliber rounds. I pulled the rounds out of the ammo belt and started throwing them to the kriegies (after making sure I stuck one in my own pocket). Some of the kriegies were crying with joy. It was a glorious sight. We took down the swastika flag and put up an American flag. It was unbelievable. We were cheering and jumping up and down. We were liberated. Thank God, WE WERE FINALLY LIBERATED!

There wasn't any champagne but we sure as hell found some food. So we celebrated by eating and eating . . . and eating some more. We found some white bread that was so light it felt like manna from heaven. Then we melted scores of chocolate D-bars and poured them over the bread. It was like eating cake!

Our stomachs hadn't been this full in years and we all got sick. The privies really got a workout. I felt the urge so bad one night that I jumped out the window and ran to the nearest privy. It was a fifty-holer, made up of two rows of seats facing each other. I rushed in the door and headed to the nearest seat. I barely made it. The noises coming out of that privy were incredible. Some guys were sitting on one John and throwing up into the next one. It was almost funny.

The next day a lieutenant- an American artillery officer- came into our camp looking for his brother, who was a POW. We found out he was bivouacked nearby and really latched on to him.

"Hey pal," I said. "How about getting us out and taking us to your bivouac so we can get some real food."

"Get your own self out," he said. "And I'll meet you at the front gate in the morning in a jeep."

We (my buddy George Stier and I) went to the front gate the next morning to see if we could talk our way out. The American officer in charge wouldn't let us. Those in charge wanted us to stay in the camp until we could be taken out en masse. Seemed it was very dangerous for Americans to be roaming around in Germany at the time. But not to be denied, we excused ourselves and snuck into a group of Polish laborers that was marching by at the time. And our new friend was there waiting for us in his jeep, just like he said he would. He took us to a farmhouse that our troops had taken over and asked us what we wanted for breakfast. "How about bacon and eggs or ham and eggs?" I asked. He was very obliging but informed us that they didn't have any eggs but asked us if pancakes would do. "Pancakes would do just fine," we said.

They were fantastic. They were soaked in butter and syrup and were just heavenly.

We spent the night there and had another round of pancakes the next morning before our new friend took us back to camp.

23

"ESCAPING" INTO MOOSBURG

George and I just couldn't stay put. So a couple of days later we cut a hole in the wire and "escaped" into Moosburg. There we found a German barracks and went souvenir hunting. The first thing I lifted was a 20-millimeter shell –just the shell, not the casing- that was being used as a paperweight. The next thing I heisted was a helmet and a bayonet. Then we strolled into town and I remember it was around dusk. All kinds of American army vehicles were moving through town. We spoke to an M.P. who was directing traffic and asked him where we could find some booze. He said, "Can't you smell it?

Just walk that way. It's about a block down on the left. I promise you, you can't miss it."

So we went down that way and the smell got stronger with every step. It was the sweet smell of wine. And how sweet it was!

When we got outside the cellar door we could hear songs resonating in German. The cellar door had a bulkhead – a sill that was raised up. We stepped up to our ankles in red wine. Using steppingstones, we got into the inner cellar and discovered kegs that were at least five feet in diameter and maybe six feet long. They were humongous. And there, on top of one of the kegs, were three liberated Dutch prisoners, drunk-and singing at the top of their lungs. They had cleverly plugged a garden hose into the bunghole of one of the kegs. The wine was coming out of the hose and going everywhere. In pidgin English they invited us to join them. So the next thing we knew George and I were drinking wine from the hose and passing it back and forth to the Dutchmen. To no avail, we tried to teach them some American songs, some Sinatra stuff. And they tried to teach us some Dutch songs, too. We all sounded pathetic, but were too drunk to care.

24

NEXT STOP: MUNICH

We staggered out of the cellar and flagged down an M.P. who was heading to Munich in a jeep. He welcomed our company, especially after he learned that we were liberated POWs.

Munich was about thirty miles south of Moosburg on the Isar River. With almost a million inhabitants, Munich was the third largest city in Germany, behind Berlin and Hamburg.

In 1923, Hitler and his supporters, who were concentrated there, staged the Beer Hall Putsch, an attempt to overthrow the Weimar Republic and seize power. The revolt failed, resulting in Hitler's arrest and the temporary crippling of the Nazi Party, which was virtually unknown outside Munich.

But the city would once again become a Nazi stronghold when the National Socialists took power in Germany in 1933.

Now, in 1945, Munich looked like a bombed out inner-city ghetto. It obviously had incurred heavy damage from allied air power. (I would later learn that Munich was hit by seventy-one air raids over a period of six years).

When we got to Munich there were M.P.s all over the place. We asked about German prisoners and if he had seen any. "Seen any," he said. "How about many, many . . . many. Lord, they've been coming in here by the battalion load – just walking in and surrendering. And they look relieved, too. Like, surrendering sure as hell beats having their heads blown off. Look over there. There's a whole battalion of krauts standing up against the wall, waiting for transportation to where the hell we're taking them."

George and I walked over and confronted a couple of them. George made one of the guys open up his coat and then he commenced to rip the German's medals right off his tunic.

In pidgin German and sign language I demanded that the other guy open his bag. Then I started kicking it, violently. I was blowing off steam and taking out my frustrations on this poor guy. But then I realized that he didn't like this war any more than I did. He's probably got some Fraulein waiting for him that he loves as much as I love Doris.

"George, this isn't right," I said. "Let's show a little class and just get the hell out of here." George agreed and we started looking for a ride back to Moosburg.

"Right over there in the parking lot you'll find plenty of vehicles," said the G.I., who was standing on the corner enjoying a cigarette.

We found one that ran on some sort a wood burner in the trunk. I couldn't figure out how it fueled the engine. I had heard of cars being run by steam, long before Daimler Benz developed the internal combustible engine. But I'd never heard of a wood-burning car.

It worked somehow, though, and George and I headed north to Moosburg. We did have a flat tire (left rear) on the trip back. We were able to change it with no problem. But I thought to myself: *God, what if a front tire had blown out and we had lost control and skidded into a tree and been killed. How cruel would that have been? After having survived a blown up B-17, being declared dead; then being declared alive and then surviving Stalag Luft III, the forced march and the flea-infested Stalag VIIA . . . only to get killed in a damn wood-burning car . . .*

George and I got back to camp around midnight and hit the sack, exhausted. The next morning we were ready to roll for another day of sightseeing, but the car had had a bad night. It had been stripped bare. It had no wheels, no battery . . ." no nothing."

Later that day I met with a War Crimes delegation to discuss my experiences with the Gestapo. I talked with a full Colonel whose name I can't remember. I told him about all the horrible things that happened to me, but he wasn't moved. He said many, many prisoners had it far worse than I did. So I humbly got up to leave. "And one more thing, Edris," said the Colonel, emphatically. "Just be thankful you weren't captured in the Pacific Theatre. I'm hearing horror stories about how those Goddamn Japs are treating our boys."

25

HOMEWARD BOUND

It was in late May of 1945 when trucks finally arrived to take us away. They started taking us up to Landshut, an airfield/town about sixty kilometers northeast of Munich.

The cynical kriegies among us quipped that we'd probably be stuck on the ground there for days. But to our surprise, we'd hardly settled onto our blankets when the first C47s roared in. One after another they came. It was like a subway system. They came in and landed and didn't even shut off their engines. They each held about thirty kriegies. They were very efficient getting us out of there.

I even got into the cockpit and flew the plane for a little while. And it was sure as hell nice to know I wasn't going to get shot down!

They took us to a little coastal town in France called Le Havre. Le Havre is in northwestern France on the mouth of the Seine River as it outlets into the Bay of Seine in the English Channel. There, the Americans had set up camps named after cigarettes. Our camp was named Lucky Strike.

Le Havre was where we were deloused. And what a sight that was. All of us kriegies were lined up on a hill, sort of like an assembly line. A group of sergeants was running the show very methodically.

I had hung on to my "family" of clothes and felt like they were a part of me. The sergeant felt differently. "Okay, lieutenant, strip and strip right now." "But . . ." I said. "These are my clothes and I don't want to give them up." "No exceptions, lieutenant. Strip down right now and put your clothes in the pile with everybody else's."

This was a battle I couldn't win so I stripped down buck-naked. And then I walked into the shower. The sergeants kept yelling at us to make it snappy but none of us wanted to get out of the shower. Once we got out we were made to put our hands over our heads and spread our legs. Then they sprayed us with some kind of delousing powder. In the next tent we were issued shoes, socks, underwear, pants and shirts . . . and duffle bags. Then we were assigned to "half tents" which were so roomy that I thought I was in the Waldorf Astoria. I actually had enough room to wiggle around. The tents even had wooden floors and partitions.

Word had come down that General Eisenhower said, "I can pick you a ship, but I don't want to hear any complaints from your congressmen about the living conditions on the ship. Is that all right?"

We all agreed that we didn't give a hoot about the conditions; we just wanted to get the hell home.

They put us on a small ship there in Le Havre that probably held about a thousand of us. They also loaded a contingent of nurses onto the ship. What a sight for sore eyes. We all rushed over to get a closer look at these young women. It's a wonder the ship didn't tip over!

Night fell as we were leaving the English Channel and I went up on the deck to walk around. There was not a cloud in the sky and the water was calm. The stars seemed brighter than I'd ever seen them before.

I pulled a letter from my duffle bag that Doris had written me on March 24, 1944.

Tears came to my eyes as I read the last part:

I love you my darling,

And I pray for you every day, and pray that you will be sent back to me before so very long.

"It won't be so very long now, honey," I remembered thinking.

"It won't be very long at all . . ."

26

CAMP KILMER TO MANHASSET

Our ship docked in Staten Island, New York in late May 1945. The next stop for us was Camp Kilmer, which was about twenty-two miles south of New York City. Camp Kilmer, named for World War I soldier/poet Joyce Kilmer, was the largest processing center for troops heading overseas and returning from World War II. During the war, two and a half million troops came through Camp Kilmer.

We arrived there in the early afternoon on a train via the Pennsylvania railroad. Once we had been herded into a large theatre and settled in, the Post Commander greeted us. "Welcome home, debarkees, he said. "And welcome to Camp Kilmer. My staff and I assure you that everything will be done for your comfort and pleasure during your short stay here."

He told us we were still in the military and to act like we were. That meant we had to be in full uniform, including caps, at all times. He also made it clear that liquor was forbidden in the camp.

"As soon as we finish your processing you can call whoever you'd like to call," he said. "And be sure to tell your loved ones not to come here as you'll see them soon."

They really treated us well there at Camp Kilmer. They made us feel like we had won the war all by ourselves. The food was good too; but our mess sargeant thought we might be offended by who was serving it: German prisoners. We didn't care, though. We just wanted some decent food for a change. We didn't care who served it.

My group commander asked me how much money I needed, and I said $300. "No problem, Edris," and he handed me 300 bucks in twenties. He made it clear, though, that it would be deducted from my back pay.

I didn't care. The only thing I cared about was getting home and reuniting with my family and Doris. And I was almost there.

> *Not iron bars, nor flashing spears,*
> *Nor land, nor sky, nor sea,*
> *Nor love's artillery of tears*
> *Can keep mine own from me.*
> **From "Madness," by Joyce Kilmer (1886-1918)**

I was hardly out of the cab when Mother came running out screaming "Junior, junior – thank God, you're home . . . I don't believe it." Right behind her were my sisters Helen and Lucille, screaming and crying. We all just stood there with our arms wrapped around each other, holding on for dear life. "I thought this day would never come," Mother said. "I'm the happiest person in Mountain Lakes, New Jersey. I'm the happiest person in the world!"

Then, here came the neighbors. Dr.Ostergren, a dentist from down the street, came bearing black market spare ribs, filet mignons and a big roast! Jokingly, he said this food is for Pete, not for any of you! Then other neighbors came with more food than you could imagine; pies, cakes . . . everything.

The celebration was on!

27

REUNION AT PENN STATION

Penn Station in midtown Manhattan is the largest and busiest train station in the United States. But on that day in early June 1945, there was hardly anyone there. It was eerily quiet for such a hustle, bustle place.

I was waiting for Doris who was on her way from Greensboro, North Carolina. She had boarded a Norfolk Southern train right after I got home; and she was running late. I asked a guy at a reception area what the delay was and he told me not to worry. "Trains just run late, sometimes," he said. Not a very good answer, I thought.

I walked around like a caged animal, smoking one cigarette after another. She was two hours late now and I was really getting jittery. Then, all of a sudden, there she was, walking across the terminal. She was glowing like an angel. She looked absolutely gorgeous. We ran full-speed into each other's arms. I picked her off the floor and we went around and around.

We were both crying like babies.

"I love you, I love you, I love you," she said. "Hold me forever, darling. Don't ever let me go."

EPILOGUE

Doris Grey Cooke and First Lieutenant Warren P. Edris were married on June 30, 1945 in Raleigh, North Carolina.

Miss Doris Grey Cooke Is To Marry Lieut. Edris June 30th

Mr. and Mrs. William Guthrie Cook of Kernersville, announce the engagement of their daughter, Doris Grey, to Lieut. Warren P. Edris Jr., A. A. F., son of Mrs. Warren P. Edris and the late Mr. Edris of Manhasset, Long Island, N. Y.

Miss Cooke is a graduate of Kernersville High School and attended Woman's College of U. N.C.

Lieutenant Edris, who has just returned from three years overseas duty, is a graduate of Oak Ridge Military Institute.

The wedding will take place the 0th of June.

DORIS GREY COOKE

Pete's credits from Oak Ridge were fully transferable and he applied to Duke University in 1946. When asked by the dean why he wanted to go to Duke Pete jokingly said, "Because of your legendary football team, The Iron Dukes, unbeaten, untied and unscored on in 1938, only to lose to Southern Cal in the 1939 Rose Bowl on the last play of the game." The dean laughed and said, "That's good enough for me, Edris. Welcome to Duke University."

Pete graduated in 1948 with a degree in business and went to work at his late father's insurance investigation business in New York City. He hated the job and in1949 rejoined the active U.S. Army Air Corps reserve unit.

He was assigned to Mitchell Field in Hempstead Plains, Long Island, N.Y., where he flew C-46s. These were cargo airlift planes like DC-3s, but twice as large. His unit, the 514th Troop Carrier Group, trained every weekend.

Mitchell Field was a thirty-mile commute from the apartment Pete and Doris were renting in Long Island City.

He was called into active duty when the Korean War broke out in June of 1950.

One of his jobs at Mitchell Field was studying flight information files. That's when he discovered the War Department's dictum that former POWs did not have to go to Korea. So Pete stayed stateside and continued doing "paper work."

One of his group's assignments during the war came from the Strategic Air Command (SAC). A B-36 group, based at Ramey Air Force Base in Puerto Rico, was being transferred to Forbes Air Force Base in Topeka, Kansas. Pete's group was assigned to haul all the ground equipment up to Forbes. SAC gave the group only a month to get the job done. It was a huge task, but the B-36 was a huge plane. It had ten engines, six pusher props and four jet engines; and weighed a whopping 410,000 pounds.

Pete and the other pilots flew individually to Miami for briefings. Then they flew non-stop to Ramey, from where they made several round trips to Kansas.

On the second or third trip, they were unable to return to Miami because of a hurricane.

During the layover in Puerto Rico, the commanding officer asked if any of the pilots would like to fly over to Haiti for some sightseeing. Pete knew from a cablegram his mother received while he was at Duke that Jacques and Suzanne were back in Haiti. Seems that the Gestapo released them and their maid after several rounds of intense interrogations. So Pete jumped at the chance to go. Maybe, just maybe, he thought, it would be possible to track down the dear people who harbored him in their Paris apartment back in 1943.

He and three of his buddies flew in a DC-3 to the "airport" at Port-O-Prince. It had a dirt field and one little building that served as its terminal.

Pete went through the building and out the back door and actually discovered a cab parked there. He asked the driver (who spoke English) if he knew a Dr. Jacques Coicou. The driver said, "Not only do I know him, I know where he lives. Come and I'll take you there."

He drove Pete and his buddies to a beautiful home where Suzanne Coicou was strolling around on the house's massive backyard patio. He got out of the cab and yelled, "Suzanne." She yelled back, "quoi?" (what?). "It's Pete," Pete yelled. Suzanne screamed, "Pete, Pete," and came running toward him. Then out came Jacques, jumping up and down in excitement. He and Suzanne tearfully took turns hugging Pete.

The reunion and celebration had begun.

Reunion in Haiti with Suzanne and Jacques

There wasn't much time to reminisce, though, because Pete and his buddies had strict orders to be back to Puerto Rico by 5:00 p.m. There was time, however, for one of his buddies to grab his camera and " capture the moment."

"Thank you two for everything," Pete said. "You will be in my thoughts and prayers forever." "Same, here," said Suzanne, with tears running down her cheeks.

Jacques put his arm around Pete and said, "Thank God for sending you to us. Again."

"And on that note," he said, "You need to get back to Puerto Rico. Come and we'll drive you to your plane."

Pete and his buddies completed their airlift mission (barely) within the thirty days allocated. After debriefings in Miami, they headed back to Mitchell Field to wait out the war.

Threats by President Eisenhower to use nuclear weapons on North Korea hastened the end of the Korean War. It officially ended with an armistice agreement signed July 27, 1953. U.S. losses were placed at 54,000 dead and 103,000 wounded.

The war provided Pete with enough flight hours to qualify as a commercial airline pilot.

He joined American Airlines in 1953 and was a co-pilot for thirteen years. He was promoted to captain in 1966 and flew for American until his retirement.

His "Farewell Flight," No. 514 from Chicago O'Hare to NYC LaGuardia, was on January 29, 1981.

Pete and Doris had two children, Warren P. III, who graduated from the Air Force Academy in Colorado Springs, Colorado; and Carolyn Ann, who graduated from Salem College in Winston-Salem, North Carolina.

Doris Cooke Edris died on April 26, 1988.

In May of the same year, at the urging of his neighbors, Pete grudgingly drove from Kernersville, North Carolina (where he and Doris had lived since 1963) to his 50th high school class reunion in Mountain Lakes, New Jersey. He choked back tears all the way.

He was reunited at the reunion with the twice-widowed Elizabeth Mae (Bette) Lees Anderson. They had gone from the fourth through the twelfth grades together.

"Wow," Bette exclaimed when she first saw Pete. "When did you GROW?"

Pete and Bette began dating right after the reunion.

They were married on September 30, 1989.

All passengers and crew members signed and personalized
this napkin for Pete on his last flight, Jan. 29, 1981.

Of the ten crew members on Pete's March 8, 1943 mission, eight became POWs, one was declared "Missing in Action" and one, Lt. Otto Buddenbaum, the pilot, was declared "Killed in Action."